A Concise

SPANISH

Grammar

A Concise
SPANISH
Grammar

R. N. de M. Leathes

John Murray

© R. N. de M. Leathes 1984

First published in 1984
by John Murray (Publishers) Ltd,
50 Albemarle Street, London W1X 4BD

Phototypeset in Great Britain
by Fakenham Photosetting Ltd
Printed and bound in Hong Kong
by Wing King Tong Co. Ltd

British Library Cataloguing in Publication Data

Leathes, R. N. de M.
    A concise Spanish grammar.
    1. Spanish language – Grammar
    i. Title
    462.2'421   PC4112
    ISBN 0 7195 3992 7

Contents

1 Pronunciation and spelling

1.1 The alphabet

a	**a**	j	**jota**	r	**erre**
b	**be**	k	**ka**	s	**ese**
c	**ce**	l	**ele**	t	**te**
ch	**che**	ll	**elle**	u	**u**
d	**de**	m	**eme**	v	**ve, uve**
e	**e**	n	**ene**	w	**ve doble, doble ve**
f	**efe**	ñ	**eñe**		(doble u – Latin America)
g	**ge**	o	**o**	x	**equis**
h	**hache**	p	**pe**	y	**i griega**
i	**i**	q	**cu**	z	**zeta**

ge mayúscula *capital G*   ge minúscula *small g*

Spanish letters are feminine.

Note that in traditional Spanish dictionaries **ch, ll** and **ñ** are treated as separate letters and follow entries for **c, l,** and **n** respectively. Thus **chalet** will follow **cuyo, pollo** will follow **polvo,** etc. Some modern dictionaries are beginning to follow English practice.

As **b** and **v** are pronounced the same or virtually the same in many parts of the Spanish speaking world, the two letters are often distinguished in the following way when spelling:

b: be de burro *or* be de Barcelona
v: ve de vaca   ve de Valencia

> ¿Cómo se escribe 'huevo'? Se escribe con hache.
> *How do you spell 'huevo' (egg)? It is spelt with an h.*

1.2 Pronunciation and spelling

a Consonants

b *&* **v** At the beginning of a word and after **m** and **n** both are pronounced like an English *b*: **barco, valle, hambre, enviar.** Elsewhere they have a sound half way between an English *b* and *v* with the lips not quite meeting: **haber, vivo, calvo, alba.**

1

c	i Before **a, o, u** or a consonant it is pronounced like the *c* in *cat*: **coche, cama, Cuba, acto**. If this *k* sound appears before **e** or **i, qu** must be used (see **q** below).
	ii Before **e, i** in northern and central Spain it is pronounced like the *th* in *thin* and in Andalucía and Latin America like the *s* in *soft*: **centro, cíudad**. Where this sound appears before **a, o, u** or a consonant, **z** is used (see below). In the combination **cc** the first **c** is hard and the second soft: **acción, lección**.
ch	As in English: **chico, leche**.
d	i At the beginning of a word and after **l** and **n** it is pronounced like an English *d*: **dar, aldea, andar**.
	ii Elsewhere the pronunciation tends towards that of the *th* in *this*: **nadar**, and in some regions it is not pronounced at all when it occurs at the end of a word or in the ending **-ado: cuidado, Madrid, usted**.
f	As in English. The combination **ph** does not exist in Spanish: **foto, elefante**.
g	i Before **e, i** it is pronounced like an English *h*, though a little stronger: **girar, gente**.
	ii Before **a, o, u** or a consonant it is a weaker version of the *g* in *garden*: **ganar, gordo, gusto, gloria**. **U** is not pronounced when it appears between **g** and **e** or **i**, but changes the sound of the **g** from that in (i) to that in (ii): **guía, guerra, distinguido**. To pronounce the **u** in this position, a diaeresis must be placed over it: **vergüenza, pingüino**.
h	Always silent in Spanish: **hombre, hijo**.
j	Pronounced like **g** (i) and appears chiefly before, **a, o, u: jarra, joven, jugo**. The main exceptions to this rule are words derived from other Spanish words written with a **j: rojo – rojizo, dejar – dejé**; words beginning with **eje-: ejemplo**; or ending in **-je, -jero, -jería: viaje, viajero, cerrajería**, *but not* **auge, cónyuge**; and the preterite of verbs with no hard *h* sound in their infinitive: **traer – traje, decir – dije**, etc. The **j** at the end of a word is often not pronounced in everyday speech: **reloj**.
k	As in English. Only used in loan words: **kilo**, etc. Otherwise the sound is rendered by **c** or **qu**.
l	As in English.
ll	In northern and central Spain it is pronounced like the *li* in *million*, in Andalucía and Latin America like a *y*, and in a few parts of South America, chiefly the River Plate region, like the *s* in *measure* or the *j* in *jacket*: **llave, calle**. An unstressed **i** never follows **ll** in Spanish: **millón**, *but* **bullía**.

2

| m | As in English. |

m   As in English.

n   As in English.

ñ   Pronounced like the *ni* in *onion*. As with **ll**, it is never followed by an unstressed **i**: **riñendo**, *but* **reñía**.

p   As in English.

q   As in English. The **u** following is always silent: **que, quince**. This is the normal representation of the *k* sound before **e, i**. Elsewhere **c** is used, as in representing the *kw* sound: **cuestión, cuando**, etc.

r   Rolled, similar to Scottish practice: **señor**. Pronounced like **rr** at the beginning of a word: **rápido**.

s   As in *same*: **casa, salir**. *Except* before **b, d, g, l, m, n**, when it is pronounced like an English *z* or the *s* in *rose*: **resbalar, desde, rasgo, asno, mismo**. In some regions, mainly in parts of Latin America, it is pronounced like a Spanish **j** before a hard consonant: **este, España**.

t   As in English.

v   See under **b**.

w   It only exists in loan words and is generally pronounced as in English: **water, whisky, weekend**. Sometimes it is rewritten as a **v** and pronounced accordingly: **vagón, vals**.

x   Generally pronounced as in English: **éxito, examen**.

y   In most parts of Spain and Latin America it is pronounced as in English. In (i) and (ii) below it is pronounced like the *s* in *measure* or the *j* in *jacket* where this treatment is given to **ll**.

It represents the unstressed **i** sound in a diphthong or triphthong:

    i at the beginning of a word, or after a prefix: **yo, yeso, cónyuge**.
    ii between two vowels: **cayó, maya** (*but* **caía**).
    iii at the end of a word: **rey, buey, soy** (*but* **leí**). (See also Diphthongs (c) below.)

The word **y** (*and*) is pronounced the same as the Spanish **i**.

z   The same pronunciation as **c** (ii). It occurs before **a, o, u**, consonants, and at the end of a word: **zapato, zorro, azufre, luz**. *Exceptions*: a few words of foreign derivation.

The main spelling changes noted above may be summarised as follows:

English sound:		*k*	*th*	*hard g*	*hard h*	*gw*
Spanish spelling:	before **a, o, u** or consonant or at end of word	c	z	g	j	gu
	before **e, i**	qu	c	gu	g(j)	gü

3

examples:

conocer	– conozco	pago	– pagué
vez	– veces	coger	– cojo
rico	– riquísimo	averiguo	– averigüé

b Vowels

a	Similar to *u* in *butter* in southern England: **bata, padre**.
e	A little sharper than the *e* in *set*: **este**.
i	Similar to the *ee* in *meet*: **hijo**.
o	Similar to the *o* in *often*: **hombre**.
u	Similar to the *oo* in *food*, but shorter: **luna**.

See also notes on **g** and **q** above.

c Diphthongs

ai/ay	Similar to the *i* in *ride*: **baile, Paraguay**.
au	Similar to the *ou* in *round*: **causa**.
ei/ey	Similar to the *ay* in *hay*: **peine, rey**.
eu	Combination of the **e** and **u** sounds described above joined together (no English equivalent): **deuda**.
ie*	Similar to the *ye* in *yet*: **cien**.
ua*	Similar to the *wo* in *won*: **cuatro**.
ue*	Similar to the *we* in *wet*: **jueves**.
uo	Similar to the *wa* in *water*: **cuota**.

* If these sounds occur at the beginning of a word they are always preceded by **h**: **hielo, huaso, huevo**. In the first case some words are written **ye-**: **yeso**.

d Double letters

These are only used in Spanish if they produce a sound different from that of the two single letters (**cc, ll, rr** above), or are pronounced separately, as in the case of **ee**: **leer, cree**, or **oo**: **sentándoos**. The combination **nn** occurs in words beginning with **n** preceded by a prefix ending in **n**, the commonest of these being **con-, en-, in-**: **connotación, ennegrecer, innecesario**.

e Capital letters

Contrary to English practice these are not used in Spanish for:

the pronoun *I* (**yo**)

days of the week and (usually) months of the year:

sábado	*Saturday*	enero	*January*

4

proper adjectives even if these are used as nouns:

los ingleses	*the English*
los países comunistas	*the Communist countries*

unless forming part of a name:

el Mercado Común	*the Common Market*

titles, except Saints:

el cardenal Cisneros, el duque de Alba, don Gumersindo, el señor Sanz

but: San Pablo   *Saint Paul*

(They are optional with royal titles and Popes.)

As in English capital letters are used at the beginning of a sentence and abbreviations:

Lunes, el dos de agosto;   Sr. D. Enrique Muñoz, etc.

In the case of titles of books, films, etc. only the first word is written with a capital letter unless names of people, places, etc. are involved:

La guerra de las galaxias	*Star Wars*
La casa de Bernarda Alba	*The House of Bernarda Alba*

The acute accent is normally omitted from capital letters:

MALAGA *for* Málaga

2　Accents

Three accents are used in modern Spanish ¨ ~ ´
For the first two see 1.2a under **g** and **ñ**.

2.1　Usage of the acute accent (´)

a　To show irregular stress

Words ending in a vowel, **n**, or **s** are stressed on the last syllable but one: **ca**sa, **li**bro, **jo**ven, **lu**nes.

Words ending in a consonant other than **n** or **s** (and including **y**) are stressed on the last syllable: co**mer**, pa**pel**, ver**dad**, es**toy**.

Where these rules are broken an accent is placed over the stressed vowel. In the case of a diphthong this is the strong vowel (**a**, **e**, **o**) or the second of the two weak vowels (**i**, **u**) together: can**ción**, escri**bí**, **lá**piz, **miér**coles, vi**vió**, cu**í**date.

b　To separate a weak vowel (*i, u*) from a strong one (*a, e, o*)

A weak vowel and a strong one normally combine to produce a diphthong and constitute one syllable: bue|no, pier|de, Jai|me, etc.

If they should be pronounced separately, an accent must be placed over the weak vowel. This applies even if the two vowels are separated by an **h**: pa|ís, cre|í, o|ído, continu|ó, hací|a, bú|ho, pro|híbe.

The accented vowel automatically carries the stress.

The same applies when a weak vowel is being isolated from the other two vowels in a triphthong: vení|ais, re|í|a.

In the combination **iu** or **ui** the second vowel normally carries the stress: di**u**rno, ru**i**do. If, however, the first vowel should be stressed and separated from the second, this must be indicated by an accent: fl**ú**|ido.

c　To distinguish between two words of different meaning or function that would otherwise be spelt the same

The accent falls on the strong vowel in the stressed syllable. These fall into three groups:

6

unaccented			**accented**	
i	*adjectives*		*pronouns*	
	mi	*my*	mí	*me*
	tu	*your*	tú	*you*
	el	*the*	él	*he*
	demonstrative adjectives		*demonstrative pronouns*	
	este	*this*	éste	*this one*
	ese	*that*	ése	*that one*
	etc.		etc.	
ii	*relative pronouns, etc.*		*interrogative and exclamatory pronouns, etc.*	
	que	*who, which*	¿qué?	*who?, which?, what a …!*
	quien	*who*	¿quién?	*who?*
	donde	*where*	¿dónde?	*where?*
	adonde	*where … to*	¿adónde?	*where … to?*
	cuando	*when*	¿cuándo?	*when?*
	cual	*which*	¿cuál?	*which?*
	cuanto	*as much as*	¿cuánto?	*how much? how!*

The accents are used in both direct and reported questions and exclamations:

¿Dónde está la leche?	*Where's the milk?*
Preguntó dónde estaba la leche	*He asked where the milk was*
¡Cuánto lo siento!	*How sorry I am!*
Dijo cuánto lo sentía	*He said how sorry he was*

iii *miscellaneous*

aun	*even*		aún	*still, yet*
como	*as, like*		cómo	*how*
de	*of, from*	*dé	*give*
mas	*but*		más	*more*
se	*(3rd person reflexive)*		sé	*I know*
si	*if*		sí	*yes,* **se** *(reflexive after preposition)*
solo	*alone*		sólo	*only*

*The accent is removed when a single object pronoun is added to it: **deme**, etc.

2.2 Accents in compound nouns

In compound nouns the first element loses any accent it had originally: **décimo + séptimo** – **decimoséptimo**, **río + platense** – **rioplatense**.

except in the case of: adverbs ending in **-mente**: fácilmente
                                  hyphenated words: soviético-japonés

Verbs accented as in 2.1a and b keep the accent when an object pronoun is added: **rompió** – **rompiólo**.

3 Punctuation

3.1 The main ways in which Spanish differs from English

a Inverted question marks and exclamation marks are used at the beginning of a question or exclamation as well as upright ones at the end. They may be found at the beginning or in the middle of a sentence and are used with the upright ones to isolate the relevant phrase (see (b) below).

b A dash is used to initiate dialogue. It is always used as the first part of the English inverted commas, but only as the second part when followed by an expression of saying, replying, etc.:

> – Eres español ¿ no? – preguntó.
> – Sí.
> – ¿ Dónde vives?
> – En un pueblo que se llama Cuacos en la provincia de Cáceres.
> – ¡No me digas! Lo conozco bien – siguió –. Mi hermana vive allí.

> *'You're Spanish, aren't you?' he asked.*
> *'Yes.'*
> *'Where do you live?'*
> *'In a village called Cuacos in the province of Cáceres.'*
> *'Well I never! I know it well,' he continued. 'My sister lives there.'*

c The comma after *Dear Sir,* in a letter becomes a colon:

Muy señor mío:	*Dear Sir,*	Querida Rosa:	*Dear Rosa,*

3.2 Punctuation used in large numbers and decimals

Spain:	2.500.000	1.975*	1,5%
Latin America:	2.500,000	1,975*	1.5%

* The full stop or comma is often used with dates as well.

3.3 Punctuation terms used in Spanish dictation

.	punto
,	coma
;	punto y coma
:	dos puntos
. . . .	puntos suspensivos
¿ ?	interrogación
¿	se abre interrogación
?	se cierra interrogación
¡ !	admiración
¡	se abre admiración
!	se cierra admiración
« »	comillas (used as '. . .')
«	se abren comillas
»	se cierran comillas
( )	paréntesis
(	se abren paréntesis
)	se cierran paréntesis
—	raya
-	guión (pequeño)

punto y aparte   *start a new paragraph*
punto final   *last full stop of passage*

4 Titles and forms of address

4.1 The Spanish forms of *you*

informal: **tú** (singular), **vosotros** (masc. plural), **vosotras** (fem. plural).
formal: **usted**, **Vd.** (singular), **ustedes**, **Vds.** (plural).

Tú and **vosotros** are used when addressing members of the family, close friends, young people, and animals. At all other times **usted** and **ustedes** are used. Each term has a corresponding set of object pronouns and possessives (7.9, 7.10, 10.1). **Usted** and **ustedes** take the third person forms throughout:

Usted **es** inglés	*You are English*
su casa y la mía	*your house and mine*
Le llamaré mañana	*I will call you tomorrow*

In Latin America **vosotros** is never used and is replaced by **ustedes**. The distinction between **tú** and **usted** is still maintained in the singular. In some regions, notably the River Plate, the word **vos** is used instead of **tú** and has a separate set of verb endings.

4.2 *Mr., Mrs., Miss*

The Spanish equivalents are: **Señor (Sr.)**, **Señora (Sra.)** and **Señorita (Srta.)**

Many people in the Spanish-speaking world use two surnames. In the case of men and the maiden name of women, the first surname is that handed down by the father, the second that handed down by the mother:

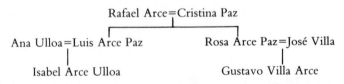

The first surname is the more important and the one normally used if either is to be used in isolation, as in conversation, or the one they will be listed under in a telephone directory, etc.

Married women may in all respectability prefer to be addressed by their maiden name right up to their dying day. Alternatively they may take on their husband's first surname in place of their mother's maiden name and preceded by **de**. Thus the woman above would be called in full:

Sra. Ana Ulloa de Arce; Sra. Rosa Arce de Villa

They would be addressed as **Sra. de Arce** and **Sra. de Villa.**
Widows often use the term **viuda** (*widow*) as a title. Thus:

la Viuda (Vda.) de Villa *or* Rosa Arce, Vda. de Villa

Mr. and Mrs. Arce   los Señores de Arce

4.3 don, doña

This is an informal title of respect given to people in authority or of some
standing in society. It must always be used with a Christian name:

don Alejandro Cambó; doña Cristina Quiroga;
¡Buenas tardes, don Alejandro!

5 Nouns

5.1 Gender

Nouns in Spanish may be either masculine or feminine.

a Feminine (main categories)

Female people, animals, etc.: **la madre, tía, reina, vaca.**
Letters of the alphabet: **la be, la ese.**
Names of islands: **Mallorca es bella.**
Countries, regions, continents, and generally towns, etc. ending in unstressed **a**: **Francia, Europa, Galicia, la Haya.**

Nouns ending in:

	main exceptions
–a	**el día, mapa, planeta, tranvía** and most words ending in **-ma: el tema, problema,** etc.
-ción, -sión and most other **-ión**	**el avión, camión, gorrión**
-dad, -tad, -tud	
-dez	
-ed	**el césped**
-ie	**el pie**
-itis	
-iz	**el lápiz, tapiz**
-sis	**el análisis, énfasis, paréntesis**
-umbre	

b Masculine

Male people, animals, etc.: **el padre, el rey, toro, gallo.**
Days of the week, months, years, numbers.
Mountains (except where the word **montaña** or **sierra** is used), seas, deserts, winds, volcanoes, points of the compass, and usually rivers: **el Sahara, el Caribe, el Sur, el Amazonas.**
Countries, regions, continents, and generally towns, etc. not ending in unstressed **a: el Canadá, el Artico, El Ferrol.**
Musical notes: **el fa.**
Trees (except **la haya, higuera, palmera**).
Other parts of speech used as nouns: **el sí, el adiós, un no sé qué,** etc.

12

Most compound nouns: **el paraguas, el pasatiempo, el altavoz.**

Nouns ending in:

	main exceptions
-o	**la mano, foto** (grafía), **moto** (cicleta)
-e (most)	**ave*, calle, carne, clase, corte, fe, fiebre, frase, fuente, gente, hambre*, leche, llave, mente, muerte, mugre, nave, nieve, noche, nube, parte, sangre, suerte, tarde, torre**
-i	**la bici** (cleta), **metrópoli**
-l	**la cal, cárcel, catedral, col, miel, piel, sal, señal**
-r	**la coliflor, flor, labor**
-u	**la tribu**
-y	**la ley**

* See 6.1.

A number of nouns may be of either gender without any change in ending. Any accompanying articles, adjectives, etc. agree with the person in question: **el/la turista, dentista, joven, estudiante, médico, colega, mártir,** etc.

The following are always feminine, even when referring to males: **estrella** (*star*), **persona, víctima, visita** (*visitor*).

5.2 Plurals

a Nouns ending in an unstressed vowel add **-s: vaca – vacas.**

Those ending in a consonant or stressed vowel add **-es: flor – flores, ciudad – ciudades, rubí – rubíes.**

exceptions:

café, canapé, mamá, papá, pie, sofá, té add **-s** only; likewise some words of foreign origin and ending in a consonant: **coñacs, clubs, jerseys,** etc.

words with a final unstressed syllable ending in **-s** do not change in the plural: **los lunes, las dosis, los paraguas,** *but*: **el dios – los dioses, el marqués – los marqueses**

Surnames are generally left in the singular, but they may be used in the plural, except if they end in **-z** or **-s**, or if they are composed of more than one name: **los Quintero(s)** *but* **los Ramírez, los García Pelayo.**

Note the spelling and accent rules (1.2a, 2.1) when forming the plural, e.g.:

la vo**z**	las vo**c**es	el autob**ú**s	los autob**u**ses
el j**o**ven	los j**ó**venes	la canci**ó**n	las canci**o**nes

With the exception of **carácter – caracteres, régimen – regímenes,** the stress never shifts in the plural.

13

b Masculine plural nouns are frequently used to describe mixed groups of both sexes: los padres (*parents*), hijos (*children*), hermanos (*brothers and sisters*), los reyes (*the king and queen*), etc.

c Some nouns may be used both in the singular and plural in Spanish but not in English:

el mueble	*piece of furniture*	los muebles	*furniture*
la noticia	*item of news*	las noticias	*the news in general*
el negocio	*a business or transaction*	los negocios	*business in general*

d Some nouns are plural in English but singular in Spanish when referring only to one unit or collective group, for example:

la limosna	*alms*	la Edad Media	*the Middle Ages*
el billar	*billiards*	la avena	*oats*
la ropa	*clothes*	el pijama	*pyjamas*
la aduana	*customs*	el estrecho	*straits*
	(e.g. at frontier)	el bosque	*woods*
el dominó	*dominoes*		

and words ending in -*ics* (the Spanish equivalent normally being **-ica**):

la física	*physics*	la política	*politics*
but: el atletismo	*athletics*		

e English often uses a plural in the following type of situation, but Spanish, applying a different logic, uses the singular:

Levantaron la cabeza   *They raised their heads*
(they only have one head each)

6 Articles

6.1 Definite article *the*

	singular	plural
masculine:	el	los
feminine:	la	las

note:

i **El** is used instead of **la** (for the sake of euphony) when it comes directly before a feminine noun beginning with a stressed **a** or **ha**:

> **el agua** *but* **la** mejor agua **la acción**
> **el ha**ba **la** mejor haba **la hormi**ga

The plural is not affected: **las** aguas, **las** habas.

ii **a** (*to*) and **de** (*of, from*) when followed by **el** become **al** and **del**:

> Le escribo **al** médico — *I write to the doctor*
> la pluma **del** general — *the pen of the general*

but:

> Llamo **a los** estudiantes — *I call the students*
> el coche **de la** tía — *the car of the aunt*

An exception is often made when **el** forms part of a name:

> el monasterio **de El** Escorial — *the monastery of El Escorial*
> con respecto **a El** Salvador — *with regard to El Salvador*

6.2 Where the definite article is used in Spanish but not in English

a Before nouns used in a general sense:

> **la** vida y **la** muerte — *life and death*
> **La** gasolina es cara — *Petrol is expensive*

except in a number of prepositional and other idioms:

> Ella es fuerte en historia — *She is good at history*
> a decir verdad — *to tell the truth*

b Before languages:

Habla bien **el** árabe	*He speaks Arabic well*
El ruso es difícil	*Russian is difficult*

except after **en**, or **de** introducing an adjectival phrase:

en alemán	*in German*
Es profesor de portugués	*He is a teacher of Portuguese*

It is usually omitted immediately after **hablar** and a few other common verbs:

Habla sueco	*He speaks Swedish*
Sabe (el) holandés	*He knows Dutch*
Estudian (el) griego	*They are studying Greek*

c Before names with titles or when qualified by an adjective:

La señora de Ortega vive aquí	*Sra. Ortega lives here*
la pobre Begoña	*poor Begoña*
el rey Carlos III	*King Charles III*

except:

with **San/Santo (a)**, **don/doña**, **fray**, **sor**, and foreign titles:
San Pedro, doña Inés, Míster Jones

when the title is in apposition:

el ministro, Sr. Arias	*the minister, Sr. Arias*

when the person is being addressed directly:

Buenos días, Señorita Urrutia	*Good morning, Srta. Urrutia*

d Before place names qualified by an adjective or adjectival phrase not forming part of the name:

la Inglaterra isabelina	*Elizabethan England*
el Madrid del siglo XX	*twentieth-century Madrid*

It is not used before the unqualified names of countries except in the following cases:

optional:

(Masculine)	Perú, Uruguay, Paraguay, Ecuador, Brasil, Canadá, Japón, Estados Unidos, Irán
(Feminine)	Argentina, India, China, Gran Bretaña

compulsory:

los Países Bajos (*the Netherlands*), el Líbano, El Salvador, el Vaticano, el Reino Unido (*United Kingdom*), and countries preceded by *Unión* or *República*, e.g.: la Unión Soviética, la República Federal Alemana

e Before certain other geographical names:

La Habana, La Coruña, La Rioja, La Mancha, La Meca, La Haya, El Cairo, etc.

f Before seasons, except after **en** or **de** used to form an adjectival phrase:

No le gusta **el** invierno   *He does not like the winter*

but:

En verano irán a Grecia   *In the summer they are going to Greece*
ropa de verano   *summer clothing*

g Before academic, religious and official buildings, meals, games, and some other nouns:

en la iglesia	*in church*
en la universidad	*at university*
a la escuela	*to school*
en el hospital	*at hospital*
a la cárcel	*to prison*
pasar por la aduana	*to go through customs*
en el tribunal	*at court*
el desayuno	*breakfast*
Juega al baloncesto	*He plays basketball*
en la cama	*in bed*
en el trabajo	*at work*
en la ciudad	*in town*
en el mar	*at sea*
en la Tierra	*on Earth*

but note:

¿Dónde está Correos?   *Where's the Post Office?*

h When the object of **tener** is a part of the body or article of clothing qualified by an adjective:

Tiene **la** nariz grande   *He has a large nose*
Tenías **la** camisa muy sucia   *Your shirt was very dirty*
(see also 7.9c)

See also: percentages (14.4b); time (14.6); age (14.8).

6.3 Where the definite article is used in English but not in Spanish

a Before a noun in apposition, unless that noun is individualised:

Londres, capital de Inglaterra   *London, the capital of England*

but:

Su tío, **el** director, es un hombre   *His uncle, the headmaster, is a*
muy simpático   *very nice man*

b In a number of set expressions, for example:

por primera vez	*for the first time*
en primer lugar	*in the first place*
a principios de	*at the beginning of*
en medio de	*in the middle of*
a orillas de	*on the shores of*

c In the following type of royal title:

Jorge sexto	*George VI*

6.4 Indefinite article *a, an, some*

	singular *(a, an)*	**plural** *(some)*
masculine:	un	unos
feminine:	una	unas

6.5 Where the indefinite article is used in Spanish but not in English

Normally before an abstract noun qualified by an adjective or adjectival phrase:

Tiene **una** habilidad sorprendente	*He has surprising ability*

6.6 Where the indefinite article is used in English but not in Spanish

a Before a noun indicating geographical origin, rank, occupation, religion, politics when used after **ser** and similar verbs:

Parece francesa	*She looks like a French woman*
Es capitán	*He is a captain*
Se hizo abogado	*He became a lawyer*
Nació rey	*He was born a king*

except where it is qualified or individualised:

Es **un** futbolista famoso	*He is a famous football player*

18

b Before nouns in apposition, unless highly individualised:

Fueron a Caldetas, pueblo catalán	*They went to Caldetas, a Catalan town*

but:

Madrid, **una** ciudad que conocemos bien	*Madrid, a city we know well*

c Before **cierto, ciento, medio, mil, otro, semejante, tal**, or with **que**:

cierta mujer	*a certain woman*
medio kilo	*half a kilo*
tal edificio	*such a building*
¡qué blusa tan bonita!	*what a pretty blouse!*

Un tal exists with the meaning *a certain*: **un tal** Sr. Balmes

d After expressions translating *as* or *for* (in the manner, capacity, etc. of; representing) followed by a noun:

Le tuvieron por espía	*They took him for a spy*
como músico	*as a musician*
Le fusilaron por traidor	*They shot him as a traitor*

e Before the object of **tener** or verbs meaning *to wear*, unless the oneness of the object is stressed or it is highly individualised:

Tengo coche	*I have a car*
Ella viste falda azul	*She is wearing a blue dress*

but:

No tienen **un** hijo sino cuatro	*They haven't got one child, but four*
Ella vestía **un** traje del siglo XIX	*She was wearing a 19th century costume*

Similarly with **con**:

Salieron con abrigo	*They left with an overcoat on*
Escribes con bolígrafo	*You write with a biro*

f After **sin**:

sin duda	*without a doubt*

g In a number of idioms:

a precio fijo	*at a fixed price*
a gran distancia	*at a great distance*
estar de buen humor	*to be in a good mood*

6.7 Usage of the neuter article 'lo'

a Before an adjective, participle or adjectival phrase to form a kind of abstract noun:

Lo interesante es que ...	*What is interesting is that ...*
Ella cree **lo** mismo	*She thinks the same*
desde **lo** alto de la colina	*from the top of the hill*
Es **lo** de siempre	*It's the same old story*
Siento **lo** ocurrido	*I'm sorry about what has happened*

In these expressions the adjective or participle is invariable.

b Before an adjective or adverb followed by **que** to translate *how* in exclamations:

Yo sé **lo** difíciles que son	*I know how difficult they are*
¿Has visto **lo** cansada que está?	*Have you seen how tired she is?*
¡Mira **lo** rápido que corre!	*Look how fast he's running!*

Note that here the adjective agrees with the noun to which it refers.

c In certain adverbial phrases, such as:

por lo menos	*at least*	por lo tanto	*therefore*
a lo mejor	*probably*	a lo largo de	*along*
a lo lejos	*in the distance*	por lo visto	*apparently*

7 Adjectives

7.1 Agreement

Adjectives agree with their noun in gender and number even if they do not stand immediately next to them:

la casa blanc**a**	*the white house*
Los libros son interesant**es**	*The books are interesting*

If the adjective is agreeing with two or more singular nouns of the same gender, a plural ending of that gender is required:

La geografía y la historia español**as**   *Spanish geography and history*

If the adjective is agreeing with both a masculine and a feminine noun, a masculine plural ending is required:

Los chicos y las chicas están conten**tos**	*The boys and girls are happy*

7.2 Feminine forms

a Adjectives ending in **–o** change to **–a**:

roj**o** – roj**a**

b The following groups add **–a**:

Adjectives of geographical origin ending in a consonant.
Those ending in **–án, –ín, –ón, –or** (except the irregular comparatives (9.1b)):

español	– español**a**	barcelonés	– barcelones**a**
holgazán	– holgazan**a**	burlón	– burlon**a**
encantador	– encantador**a**		

c The remainder do not change:

tu perro – **tu** camisa, el general **belga** – la monja **belga**, el lápiz **verde** – la pluma **verde**, el estudiante **feliz** – la enfermera **feliz**, el cónsul **iraquí** – la embajada **iraquí**, el **mejor** capítulo – la **mejor** novela

7.3 Plural forms

a Adjectives ending in an unstressed vowel add **-s**:

verde – verde**s**, tonto – tonto**s**, buena – buena**s**, su – su**s**

b Those ending in a stressed vowel or consonant add **-es**:

hindú – hindú**es**, marroquí – marroquí**es**, regular – regular**es**, fácil – fácil**es**, francés – frances**es**

Note that those in 7.2b above will therefore have a masculine plural ending in **-es** and a feminine plural ending in **-as**:

español**es** – español**as**, encantador**es** – encantador**as**

The usual spelling and accent rules (1.2a, 2.1) apply when forming the feminine and plural:

inglés – ingl**esa**, ingl**eses**, ingl**esas**; feliz – feli**ces**

7.4 Adjectives never changing in the feminine or plural

These are other parts of speech used adjectivally, such as nouns used as colours, and compound adjectives:

las corbatas **rosa**	*the pink ties*
los coches **azul oscuro**	*the dark blue cars*
coches **cama**	*sleeping cars*

In the case of some well used compound nouns this rule is now being broken, for example:

lenguas **madres**	*mother tongues*
ciudades **satelites**	*satellite towns*

7.5 Shortened forms

a The following adjectives drop the final **-o** before a masculine singular noun: **bueno, malo, alguno, ninguno, primero, tercero, postrero, uno** (and compounds in front of masculine plural nouns):

el **tercer** día, el **primer** libro, **algún** día, **un buen** jefe, **veintiún** árboles

b **Santo** changes to **San**, except with saints' names beginning **Do-** or **To-**:

San Miguel, **Santo** Domingo, **Santo** Tomás

Santa is not affected: **Santa** María

c **Grande** usually becomes **gran** before singular nouns of either gender:

El **gran** presidente, la **gran** actriz

d **Ciento** becomes **cien** except before a number smaller than itself:

cien mil	*100,000*	**cien** barcos	*100 boats*
Compró **cien**	*He bought 100*		

but: **ciento** dos   *102*

e **Cualquiera** and **cualesquiera** usually drop the final -a before nouns of either gender:

cualquier mes, **cualquier** situación

7.6 Position of adjectives

Adjectives in Spanish normally follow the noun they qualify, but this rule is often broken for stylistic reasons as well as in the cases given below.

a **Adjectives preceding the noun**

i Possessives, demonstratives, numerals (with a few exceptions – see 7.10, 14.2).

ii Other adjectives of quantity such as **alguno**, **cada**, **demás**, **bastante**, **demasiado**, **mucho**, **poco**, **cuanto**, **todo**, **ninguno**, **otro**, **tal**:

cada semana	*each week*
mucha agua	*a lot of water*
demasiado pan	*too much bread*

note: **otro** normally precedes any numeral or adjective of quantity used with it:

otras muchas mujeres	*many other women*

Alguno precedes the noun unless used negatively:

algunos caballos	*some horses*

but:

sin dinero **alguno**	*without any money*
(see 12.2c)	

iii Adjectives used figuratively:

la **triste** verdad	*the sad truth*
un **viejo** amigo mío	*an old friend of mine*

but:

su cara **triste**	*his sad face*
un coche **viejo**	*an old car*

23

iv Adjectives used with names: el **amable** don Joaquín
   except where they have become part of that name: Alfonso **el Sabio**

v Adjectives that describe a noun without identifying it often come first:

   el **famoso** pintor, Francisco Goya y Lucientes
   the famous painter, Francisco Goya y Lucientes
   (The painter is identified by his name, not the fact that he is famous.)

   la **blanca** nieve de la sierra
   the white snow of the mountains
   (The snow is defined by its location, not its natural colour.)

b **Adjectives following a noun**

i Defining adjectives (such as normally colours, nationalities, those describing physical features, etc.):

los televisores **japoneses**	*Japanese television sets*
la manzana **verde**	*the green apple*
la torre **alta**	*the high tower*

ii Compound adjectives and usually those qualified by an adverb:

una familia **bastante rica**	*quite a rich family*
una alfombra **marrón oscuro**	*a dark brown carpet*
la iglesia **más importante**	*the most important church*

iii A number of common adjectives, such as **bueno, malo, joven, viejo, grande** and **pequeño** may be used before or after the noun.

   They generally come before in set expressions and come after for emphasis:

Buenos días	*Good morning*
Buen viaje	*Have a good trip*
Hace **mal** tiempo	*The weather is bad*
mala suerte	*bad luck*
los **viejos** tiempos	*old times*
una taza **pequeña** *or* una **pequeña** taza	*a small cup*
una película **mala**	*a (really) bad film*
un viaje **bueno**	*a (really) good trip*

   contrast:

   El estudiante **joven** es inteligente
   The young student (as opposed to any other) *is intelligent*

   El **joven** estudiante allí se llama Luis
   The young student over there is called Luis
   (Here the student is identified by his location, not by his age.)

   See also irregular comparatives (9.1b).

c Position of adjectives when two adjectives are used with a noun

When both adjectives are of equal importance they usually follow the noun and are joined by **y**:

una señorita **guapa y simpática**   *a nice attractive young lady*

Otherwise the adjective less closely related to the noun usually comes first:

una **hermosa** playa andaluza   *a beautiful Andalucian beach*

unless one adjective is so close to the noun as to form a kind of compound noun:

los jefes **sindicales italianos**   *the Italian trade union leaders*

These rules do not apply where one or more of the adjectives in (a) are being used:

sus primeros esfuerzos   *his first efforts*
aquel gran capitán   *that great captain*

In the combination: noun – adjective – adjectival phrase or clause, the adjective usually precedes the noun:

una **inmensa** bocanada de viento   *a great gust of wind*

7.7 Some adjectives change their meaning according to their position.

For example:

	before noun	**after noun**
antiguo	*former*	*old, ancient*
cierto	*a certain (unspecified)**	*definite*
diferente	*various*	*different*
grande	*great, grand*	*big*
medio	*half**	*average*
mismo	*same*	*-self, precisely*
nuevo	*new, another, fresh*	*brand new*
pobre	*poor (unfortunate)*	*poor (penniless)*
puro	*sheer, mere*	*pure (untainted)*
varios	*several*	*various, different*
viejo	*old (long known, etc.)*	*old (aged)*

*See 6.6c.

7.8 Adjectives used as nouns

Adjectives in Spanish may be used as a kind of noun. They agree in the usual way:

¿Qué bufanda le gusta? Me gusta **la azul.**   *Which scarf do you like? I like the blue one.*

un barco inglés y **uno francés**   *an English boat and a French one*
(Note that **uno** does not drop its **o** when used in this way.)

los ricos   *the rich*
la vieja   *the old woman*

7.9 Possessive adjectives (weak forms)

	singular		plural	
	masculine	*feminine*	*masculine*	*feminine*
my	mi	mi	mis	mis
your (of **tú**)	tu	tu	tus	tus
his, her, its, *your* (of **usted**)	su	su	sus	sus
our	nuestro	nuestra	nuestros	nuestras
your (of **vosotros**)	vuestro	vuestra	vuestros	vuestras
their, *your* (of **ustedes**)	su	su	sus	sus

a All possessive adjectives agree in gender and number with the nouns they qualify, not the owner. The weak forms always precede the noun:

mis camisas   *my shirts*
nuestro perro   *our dog*
Ella necesita **sus** cuadernos   *She needs her exercise books*

b As **su(s)** can mean *his, her, your* (of **Vd.**, **Vds.**) or *their*, clarification is needed unless the meaning is obvious from the context (as in the last example above). This is done in the following way:

Tengo **la** pluma **de él**   *I have his pen*
instead of: Tengo **su** pluma

Vimos **al** padre **de ellos**   *We saw their father*
instead of: Vimos a **su** padre

Conoce a **los** hermanos **de Vd.** *He knows your brothers*
instead of: Conoce a **sus** hermanos

Alternatively **su** may be retained instead of the definite article.
Thus: Conoce a **sus** hermanos **de Vd.**

c When parts of the body or articles of clothing are the object of a verb, possession is shown:

i   by a reflexive pronoun if they belong to the subject:

Se quitó el impermeable   *He took his (own) raincoat off*
Me he roto la pierna   *I have broken my leg*

ii otherwise by an indirect object pronoun:

Tu madre **te** lavará la cara	*Your mother will wash your face*
Le aprietan los zapatos	*His shoes are pinching him*

Where ownership is clear, the object pronoun is frequently omitted:

Abrió la boca	*He opened his mouth*
Lleva el sombrero así	*He wears his hat like this*

7.10 Possessive adjectives (strong forms)

	singular		plural	
	masculine	*feminine*	*masculine*	*feminine*
my/mine	mío	mía	míos	mías
your(s) (of **tú**)	tuyo	tuya	tuyos	tuyas
his, her(s), its, *your(s)* (of **Vd.**)	suyo	suya	suyos	suyas
our(s)	nuestro	nuestra	nuestros	nuestras
your(s) (of **vosotros**)	vuestro	vuestra	vuestros	vuestras
their(s) *your(s)* (of **Vds.**)	suyo	suya	suyos	suyas

a They agree in the same way as the weak forms above (7.9).

b They are used:

i after a noun when addressing people figuratively or literally:

hijo **mío**	*my son*
¡Madre **mía**!	*Good heavens!*
¡Dios **mío**!	*My God!*
Muy señor **mío**	*Dear Sir* (in letters)

except:

when addressing military superiors: Sí, **mi** capitán
terms of affection: **mi** corazón, **mi** vida, etc.

ii in the following expression:

un amigo **mío**	*a friend of mine*
algo **tuyo**	*something of yours*

(Note omission of **de**.)

iii after the verb **ser**:

Este lápiz es **nuestro**	*This pencil is ours*

For emphasis the definite article is placed in front:

Este lápiz es **el** nuestro, ése es **el** vuestro	*This pencil is ours, that one is yours*

c The clarification of **suyo** is similar to that of **su** above:

el amigo **de ella**   *the friend of hers*
(*for* el amigo **suyo**)
Este gato es **de Vd.**   *This cat is yours*

or:

Este gato es **el de Vd.** (in the emphatic form)

7.11 Demonstrative adjectives

		masculine	feminine
this		este	esta
these		estos	estas
that	{far from speaker but	ese	esa
those	near person addressed}	esos	esas
that	{far from both speaker	aquel	aquella
those	and person addressed}	aquellos	aquellas

The demonstrative adjectives normally precede the noun they qualify (as 7.10 above).

8 Adverbs

8.1 Formation

a Many adverbs are formed by adding **-mente** to the feminine form of the adjective:

fácil   fácilmente   franco   francamente

Any accents on the adjective are retained as the suffix is stressed independently.

When two or more such adverbs are joined by a conjunction, the **-mente** is omitted from all but the last:

Se lo dijo **severa** pero   *He told him so severely but politely*
cortésmente

b As the adverbs ending in **-mente** are often rather cumbersome, adjectives are frequently used instead:

Los compramos muy **barato**   *We bought them very cheap*
Ella corre **rápido**   *She runs fast*

In some cases they agree:

Vivieron **contentos**   *They lived happily*
Vendió **cara** su vida   *He paid for his life dearly*

Alternatively an adverbial phrase can be used:

con frecuencia   *frequently*
por fin   *finally*
con cuidado   *carefully*

de $\left\{\begin{array}{l}\text{una manera}\\ \text{un modo}\end{array}\right\}$ muy audaz   *very audaciously*

c Irregular adverbs

bueno   *good*   bien   *well*
malo   *bad*   mal   *badly*

recientemente shortens to **recién** before a past participle:

los **recién** casados   *the newly married couple*

In Spanish America it may be used at other times as well:

Recién salió   *He left a short while ago*

8.2 Position

a An adverb modifying a verb may either precede it for emphasis or follow immediately after it:

Siempre está hablando por
teléfono con su novio
Conocemos **bien** a Rosalía

*She is always talking on the phone
to her boyfriend*
We know Rosalia well

b An adverb generally precedes any adjective or other adverb it modifies:

Vive **muy** cerca
Son **demasiado** caros

He lives very near
They are too expensive

c The following adverbs always precede any other they accompany:
aquí, allí (ahí), ayer, hoy, mañana:

allí mismo   *right there*   **mañana** temprano   *early tomorrow*
aquí cerca   *near here*

9 Comparisons

9.1 Comparison of adjectives

a Regular comparatives

positive	comparative	superlative
fácil	más fácil	el más fácil
easy	*easier*	*(the) easiest*
	menos fácil	el menos fácil
	less easy	*the least easy*

The adjectives and articles agree in the usual way:

Estos ejercicios son fáciles, pero el que hice ayer es **el más fácil** de todos
These exercises are easy, but the one I did yesterday is the easiest of all

El edificio nuevo es **menos feo**
The new building is less ugly

Su abuela es la mujer **más vieja** de la ciudad
His grandmother is the oldest woman in the town
(Note that *in* after a superlative is translated by **de**.)

b Irregular comparatives

bueno	mejor	el mejor	*good*	*better*	*(the) best*
malo	peor	el peor	*bad*	*worse*	*(the) worst*
grande	mayor	el mayor		(see below)	
pequeño	menor	el menor		(see below)	

Mejor and **peor** are usually placed before the noun:

| la **mejor** película | *the best film* |
| el **peor** vino | *the worst wine* |

Más (or **menos**) **grande** and similarly **pequeño** are used mostly for physical size:

| Esta vaca es **más grande** que la otra | *This cow is bigger than the other one* |
| Aquel cuchillo es **el más pequeño** | *That knife over there is the smallest* |

Mayor and **menor** are used above all for age, degrees of importance and

abstract size. They come before the noun when expressing degrees of importance, abstract size or relative quantities:

No cabe la **menor** duda	*There is not the slightest doubt*
La **mayor** parte	*The greater part, the majority*

and after the noun when expressing age or seniority and in a few set expressions:

Miguel es el hijo **mayor**	*Michael is the eldest son*
la calle **mayor**	*the High Street*
la plaza **mayor**	*the main square*

Other irregular comparatives:

anterior	*previous*	posterior	*subsequent, later*
exterior	*external, exterior*	interior	*internal, inside*
superior	*upper*	inferior	*lower*

these usually come after the noun:

la semana **anterior**	*the previous week*
la habitaciones **interiores**	*the inside rooms*

c **The absolute superlative (*very*, *most*, *extremely*, etc. + adjective)**

This may be formed by adding **-ísimo** to the adjective after removing the final
vowel where necessary, e.g.:

viejo	viejísimo	poco	poquísimo*
difícil	dificilísimo*	feroz	ferocísimo*
rápido	rapidísimo*	largo	larguísimo*

* Note the new accentuation and the usual spelling changes.

Es un coche **rapidísimo**	*It is an extremely fast car*
la leonesa **ferocísima**	*the very fierce lioness*

There are some irregular forms, e.g.:

amable	amabílisimo
nuevo	novísimo

Alternatively **muy** (*very*) may be placed in front of the adjective:

La novela es **muy** interesante	*The novel is very interesting*

except in the case of **mucho**:

Había **muchísima** gente allí	*There were very many people there*
Le gusta **muchísimo**	*He likes it very much*

mucho translates *very* on its own:

¿Está enojado? Sí, pero no **mucho**.	*Is he annoyed? Yes, but not very.*

9.2 Comparison of adverbs

a Regular comparison

In both the comparative and superlative **más** is added before the adverb:

Pedro corre **más** rápido	*Peter runs faster*
El que corre **más** rápido es José	*The one who runs the fastest is José*

Lo is added before a superlative when there is some further qualification:

Antonio corrió **lo** más rápido que pudo	*Anthony ran as fast as he could*

b Irregular comparison

bien	mejor	(lo) mejor		*well*	*better*	*(the) best*
mal	peor	(lo) peor		*badly*	*worse*	*(the) worst*
mucho	más	(lo) más		*much*	*more*	*(the) most*
poco	menos	(lo) menos		*little*	*less*	*(the) least*

note:

más bien exists and means *rather* when correcting or modifying a previous statement:

Yo diría que es **más bien** fornido que gordo	*I would say he is stocky rather than fat*

más and **menos** are invariable when used as adjectives:

Ellos tienen **más** muebles	*They have more furniture*
Vd. ha gastado **menos** dinero	*You have spent less money*

9.3 Further expressions of comparison

a *More/less than* **más/menos que**

i **Más que** and **menos que** are used except in cases (ii) and (iii) below:

Rosa es **más** encantadora **que** Montserrat	*Rosa is more charming than Montserrat*
Paco come **menos que** Enrique	*Paco eats less than Enrique*
Maribel estudia **más** asignaturas **que** ella	*Maribel is studying more subjects than her*

ii **Más de** and **menos de** are used before numbers:

Tiene **más de** cinco hermanas	*He has more than five sisters*

note that this does not apply to the expression **no . . . . . más que** (*only*):

No tenemos **más que** cien pesetas	*We only have a hundred pesetas*

iii Before a finite verb **más/menos de** (def. art.) **que** is used. Where a noun is being compared, the article agrees with it, otherwise **lo** is used:

Gasta **menos** dinero **del que** gana	He spends less money than he earns
Tenemos **más** manzanas **de las que** podemos. comer	We have more apples than we can eat
Ella es **más** astuta **de lo que** parece	She is more astute than she appears
Sabe **más de lo que** Vd. cree	He knows more than you think

Más (or **menos**) **que** may be used on its own as in (a) in spoken Spanish.

b *As ..... as* **tan ..... como**

Esta casa es **tan** moderna **como** aquélla	This house is as modern as that one

c *As much/many ..... as* **tanto ..... como**

Tanto agrees when used adjectivally:

Esta sala no tiene **tantos** cuadros **como** ésa
This room has not got as many pictures as that one

Vds. no beben **tanto como** ellos
You do not drink as much as them

d *The more/less ... the more/less* **cuanto más/menos ... tanto más/menos**

Cuanto and **tanto** agree when used adjectivally. **Tanto** may be omitted:

Cuanto más come, **tanto más** engorda
The more he eats, the fatter he gets

Cuantos más coches venden **tanto más** feliz será el gerente
The more cars they sell, the happier the manager will be

e *So ... that* **tan ... que**

Estaba **tan** enfermo **que** le llevaron al hospital
He was so ill that they took him to hospital

f *More and more/less and less* **cada vez más/menos**

Está trabajando **cada vez menos** en la oficina
He is working less and less in the office

A ella le gusta la música **cada vez más**
She likes music more and more

g *Too (much/many) ... to* **demasiado ... para**

Demasiado agrees when used as an adjective:

Tiene **demasiada** inteligencia **para** dejarse engañar así
He is too intelligent to allow himself to be deceived like that

Es **demasiado** temprano **para** cenar
It is too early to have supper

h *Enough ... to* **bastante ... para**

Bastante agrees when used as an adjective:

Tiene **bastante** dinero **para** comprar la finca
He has enough money to buy the farm

No se siente **bastante** bien **para** ir a la reunión
He does not feel well enough to go to the party

Bastante also means *quite, quite a bit, quite a few*. In this context it is followed by **que** + infinitive:

Hace **bastante** calor
It is quite hot

Había **bastante** ruido
There was quite a bit of noise

Tengo **bastantes** cosas **que** hacer
I have quite a few things to do

10 Pronouns

10.1 Personal pronouns

	subject	direct object	indirect object	reflexive
	(I, etc.)	*(me, etc.)*	*(to me, etc.)*	*(myself, etc.)*
I	yo	me	me	me
you*	tú	te	te	te
he, it (masc.)	él	lo		
she, it (fem.)	ella	la	le	se
you*	usted (Vd.)	lo, la		
we (masc.)	nosotros	nos	nos	nos
we (all fem.)	nosotras			
you* (masc.)	vosotros	os	os	os
you* (all fem.)	vosotras			
they (masc.)	ellos	los		
they (all fem.)	ellas	las	les	se
you*	ustedes (Vds.)	los, las		

* For the translation of *you* into Spanish see 4.1.

Nosotros, vosotros and **ellos** may also be used for mixed groups of both sexes.

10.2 Use of subject pronouns

a Subject pronouns are only used with a verb when added either for clarity (particularly in the case of the third person), or for emphasis:

Eres estudiante	*You are a student*
Somos turistas	*We are tourists*
Yo soy español, pero **él** es mejicano	*I am Spanish, but he is Mexican*

b **Vd.** and **Vds.** should always be put in for politeness whether otherwise needed or not.

c The words *it* or *they*, when referring to things, are never translated when they are the subject:

¿Qué es? Es una oveja.	*What is it? It is a sheep.*
¿Qué son? Son corbatas.	*What are they? They're ties.*

10.3 Position and order of subject and object pronouns

a The order of object pronouns is always the same:

reflexive – indirect – direct (R – I – D)

b Word order in statements (except where an infinitive or present participle is being used on its own – see (c) below):

1	2	3	4	5	6	7
subject	1st negative	reflexive	indirect object	direct object	verb	2nd negative

examples:

1 5 6
El me ve   *He sees me*

1   3   6
Nosotros nos lavamos   *We wash ourselves*

1 4 5   6
Yo te lo he dado   *I have given it to you*

1   5   6
Ella los está llamando   *She is calling them*

1   2 4 5   6
Vds. no me la mostraron   *You did not show it to me*

1   2   5   6
Vosotros nunca los podéis encontrar   *You can never find them*

1 2 4 5   6   7
Tú no nos lo prestas nunca   *You never lend it to us*

The negatives are explained more fully in Chapter 12.

c Word order with infinitives and present participles

When an infinitive or present participle is being used on its own, the object pronouns are joined on to the end of the verb as follows:

afeitar**se**	*to shave (oneself)*	comiéndo**lo**	*eating it*
enviándo**melo**	*sending it to me*	dár**telo**	*to give it to you*

Accents are required except where only one pronoun is added to the infinitive.

Where an infinitive or present participle depends on a previous verb, the object pronouns may be used either before the first verb or after the second:

Me lo quiere dar ⎱
Quiere dár**melo** ⎰   *He wants to give it to me*

Le voy a escribir ⎱
Voy a escribir**le** ⎰   *I am going to write to him*

Lo está bebiendo ⎱
Está bebiéndo**lo** ⎰   *He is drinking it*

d Word order with imperatives/commands

Object pronouns come before negative imperatives, but after positive imperatives. The subject pronoun always follows the imperative if it is needed for
emphasis:

No **lo** prestes	*Don't lend it*
Préstalo	*Lend it*
¡Oye **tú**!	*Hey, you!*

e Word order in questions

The subject pronoun, if needed, may be placed either at the beginning of the
phrase or immediately after the verb. Object pronouns are not affected:

Vd. ¿cuándo llegó? ⎱	*When did you arrive?*
¿Cuándo llegó **Vd.**? ⎰	
¿Han pagado **Vds.**?	*Have you paid?*
¿Cuándo me lo puede hacer **Vd.**?	*When can you do it for me?*

Note that two interdependent verbs may never be separated. Quite often
questions are structured the same way as statements, the only difference being
the rising intonation:

¿Ella ha estado enferma?	*Has she been ill?*

f In literary Spanish object pronouns may be found after any of the tenses in
10.3b, especially at the beginning of a sentence:

Habíale prometido doña	*Doña Perfecta had promised him . . .*
Perfecta . . . (Galdós)	

10.4 Further notes on object pronouns

a Combination of two 3rd person object pronouns

Where two 3rd person object pronouns are combined, the first becomes **se**:

yo **se** lo doy { *for:* yo **le** lo doy   *I give it to him/her/you*
              or: yo **les** lo doy   *I give it to them/you*

b Clarification of 3rd person indirect object pronouns

As: **le** can mean *to him, to her, to you* (**Vd.**)
     les can mean *to them* (masc. or fem.) or *to you* (**Vds.**)
     se can mean all of the above,
a él *to him*, **a ella** *to her*, etc. is added to the phrase, usually after the verb, where
clarification is needed:

Yo le escribo **a ella**   *I write to her*
Yo se lo doy **a ellos**   *I give it to them*

Note that the indirect object pronoun must still be retained even if it no longer seems necessary.

c **Le** is used in many parts of the Spanish speaking world instead of **lo** where **lo** refers to people. **Les** is likewise used instead of **los**, but in fewer areas:

Le/lo veo mañana   *I'm seeing him tomorrow*
Les/los conocimos en Madrid   *We met them in Madrid*

d The indirect object pronouns often translate *for me*, etc. as well as *to me*, etc:

Te ha comprado un regalo   *He has bought a present for you*
Me lo preparará esta tarde   *He will prepare it for me this afternoon*

The indirect object is often disguised in English, thus the first sentence could also be translated: *He has bought you a present.*

e Where a noun object precedes the verb in Spanish it must be represented by the appropriate object pronoun as well:

La región **la** conocemos muy bien,   *We know the region well, but not*
    pero la ciudad no   *the city*
Al tío **le** visitamos ayer   *We visited the uncle yesterday*

This rule is often applied when a noun follows the verb as an indirect object:

Le va a telefonear **a María**   *She is going to phone María*

f Indirect object pronouns may be used instead of possessive adjectives with parts of the body or clothing (see 7.9c):

Me duele el brazo   *My arm aches*

g Object pronouns may not be used when isolated from the verb:

¿A quién viste, a **él** o a **ella**? A **él**.   *Whom did you see, him or her? Him.*

h Indirect object pronouns are not generally used after verbs implying motion:

Iremos a **él**   *We will go to him*

i The neuter object pronoun **lo** replaces a noun or adjective as the complement of a verb:

¿Es Vd. australiano? Sí, **lo** soy.   *Are you Australian? Yes I am.*

10.5 Reflexive pronouns

The use of these is covered extensively in 16.27. See also below (10.6).

10.6 Pronouns after prepositions

a These are the same as the subject pronouns, except for **mí** (*me*) and **ti** (*you* singular):

para **mí**	*for me*	detrás de **nosotros**	*behind us*
hacia **él**	*towards him*		

b Reflexive pronouns used after a preposition:

Mí, **ti**, **nosotros** and **vosotros** as above
sí for all third person pronouns

Estaba leyendo para **mí**	*I was reading to myself*
El está hablando para **sí**	*He is talking to himself*
Colocó el cojín debajo de **sí**	*He placed the cushion under him(self)*

c **Con** combines with **mí**, **ti** and **sí** to form **conmigo**, **contigo**, **consigo**:

Ven **con nosotros**	*Come with us*
Llegaron **con ella**	*They arrived with her*
Lo trajo **consigo**	*He brought it with him*
Charlaron **conmigo**	*They chatted with me*

d A subject pronoun is used after the following prepositions:

entre *between, among*; **hasta**, **incluso** *even, including*; **salvo**, **menos** *except*; **según** *according to* (the same applies to the conjunctions **y**, **o** and **que**):

entre **tú** y **yo**	*between you and me*
hasta **ella**	*even she*
todos menos **nosotros**	*everybody except us*

e **Ello** *it, that* is used after a preposition when referring to an idea or statement and not a concrete noun:

Con respecto a **ello**	*As far as that is concerned*
¡A **ello**!	*Let's get down to it!*

f These pronouns used after prepositions may also be used for emphasis or to clarify object pronouns (see 10.4b):

A mí no me gusta, pero **a él** sí	*I don't like it, but he does*
¿Qué te pasa **a ti**?	*What's the matter with you?*
Le está escribiendo **a él**, no **a ella**	*He is writing to him, not her*

g They replace an indirect object pronoun when there is a direct object pronoun in the first or second person:

Nos dirigieron **a Vd.**   *They directed us to you*

and generally when a reflexive verb takes **a**:

Me refiero a **ella**   *I am referring to her*
Se rindieron a **ellos**   *They surrendered to them*

h **A él**, **de él**, do not contract as is the case with the definite article (6.1).

10.7 Relative pronouns

	singular	**plural**
who (subject)	que	que
whom (direct object)	{ que* a quien	que* a quienes
to whom	a quien	a quienes
of whom	{ de que de quien	de que de quienes
whose	cuyo	cuyo

* **Que** is used more frequently than **a quien(es)**.

	singular and plural
which (subject)	que
which (direct object)	que
to which	a que
of which	de que
whose	cuyo

These forms may refer to people or things of either gender.
Cuyo agrees adjectivally with the noun it qualifies, NOT with the owner.

a The relative pronoun may never be left out in Spanish:

la madre **que** está aquí	*the mother who is here*
el médico **que** (**a quien**) vio ayer	*the doctor he saw yesterday*
la casa **que** están construyendo	*the house which they are building*
las chicas **a quienes** estábamos hablando	*the girls we were talking to*
los países **de que** estás escribiendo	*the countries you are writing about*
el soldado **cuya** novia está enferma	*the soldier whose girl friend is ill*

41

b When the relative is separated from the word to which it refers, or if it is unclear, it is replaced by **el cual** or **el que**, both of which agree:

El perro de mi hermana, **el cual** (*or* **el que**) se llama Pepito, es negro
My sister's dog, which is called Pepito, is black
(**Que** would mean that the sister, not the dog, is called Pepito.)

Las hijas de don Pablo, **las cuales** (*or* **las que**) iban a visitaros esta tarde, tuvieron que ir a ver a su tía
The daughters of don Pablo, who were going to visit you this afternoon, had to go and see their aunt

El cual, etc. may also be used where there is a weak link between the relative and its antecedent:

Luego llamaron al Sr. Ribeiro, **el cual**, a pesar de ser el gerente, les dijo que no sabía nada del asunto
They rang Sr. Ribeiro, who, despite being the manager, told them he knew nothing about the matter

c **Que** and **quien** are generally used after the prepositions **a**, **de**, **con** and **en**. After other prepositions **el que** or **el cual**, etc. are used instead:

La mujer **con quien** vino es actriz
The woman with whom he came is an actress

El piso **en que** ella vive es moderno
The flat she lives in is modern

el árbol debajo **del cual** estaba sentado el pastor
the tree under which the shepherd was sitting

la calle por **la cual** está corriendo el chico
the street the boy is running along

En que may be replaced by **en donde** or **donde** when translating *where*.
En que may also be used instead of **cuando** (*when*):

la semana **en que** llegaste
the week you arrived

d Compound relatives *he who, she who, the one who/which*, etc. are translated by **el que**, etc:

Esta moto es **la que** quiero comprar
This motorbike is the one I want to buy

¿Conoces el edificio? **El que** está enfrente del banco.
Do you know the building? The one which is opposite the bank.

Los que han terminado su trabajo pueden leer
Those who have finished their work may read

Quien may also be used to translate *he who*, etc., and also *whoever*:

Ella era **quien** fue a Alemania
She was the one who went to Germany

Quien dice eso debe estar loco
Whoever says that must be mad

e The neuter **lo que** translates *what* or *which* when referring to an idea, statement or undefined noun or activity:

No sabe **lo que** estáis haciendo
He doesn't know what you are doing

Lo que vimos esta mañana era una maravilla
What we saw this morning was marvellous

No dijo nada, **lo que** les pareció muy raro
He did not say anything, which they thought most odd

In the last type of expression **lo cual** may also be used.

f *All that* is translated by **todo lo que.**

All who, all those which are translated by **todos los que** or **todas las que**:

Explicó **todo lo que** pasó
He explained all that happened

Todos los que fueron a la fiesta se divirtieron mucho
All who went to the party enjoyed themselves a lot

¿Cuáles botellas? **Todas las que** están en la barra.
Which bottles? All those on the bar.

g **El** (etc.) **de** translates *the one of, that of, X's one*:

estos lápices y **los de** Tomás
these pencils and Thomas's

esta foto y **la de** su hija
this photo and that of his daughter

El programa de hoy es mejor que **el de** ayer
Today's programme is better than yesterday's

10.8 Possessive pronouns

Possessive pronouns are the same as the strong forms of the possessive adjectives (7.10) and are always accompanied by the definite article:

nuestra oficina y **la suya** or **la de él**	*our office and his*
tus bolígrafos y **los míos**	*your biros and mine*

10.9 Demonstrative pronouns

	masculine	feminine	neuter		masculine	feminine
this	éste	ésta	esto	*these*	éstos	éstas
that	{ ése	ésa	eso	*those*	{ ésos	éstas
	{ aquél	aquélla	aquello		{ aquéllos	aquéllas

The difference between **ése** and **aquél** is the same as between the corresponding adjectives (7.11).

Note the accent on the masculine and feminine forms:

este almacén y **aquél**	*this store and that one*
esa cuchara y **ésta**	*that spoon and this one*

The neuter forms may only refer to ideas, statements, etc. and never to specified nouns:

¿Has visto **esto**?	*Have you seen this?*
Eso no le gusta	*He doesn't like that*
esto de los cheques	*this business about the cheques*

Aquél can also translate *the former*, and **éste** *the latter*:

Estaban hablando con Carmen y Rocío, **ésta** les dijo...	*They were talking to Carmen and Rocío, the latter said to them...*

11 Indefinite adjectives and pronouns

11.1 Algo, alguien, alguno

a Algo *something, anything*

¿Buscas **algo**?	*Are you looking for anything?*
Algo ha ocurrido	*Something has happened*

In front of an adjective or adverb it can mean *somewhat, a little*:

Está **algo** enojado   *He is a little annoyed*

Algo de means *a little* (quantity):

Sabe **algo de** latín   *He knows a little latin*

b Alguien *someone, anyone*

Hay **alguien** en el vestíbulo   *There is someone in the hall*

As an object it may be preceded by personal **a** (19.5c):

Encontramos **a** alguien en la calle   *We met someone in the street*

c Alguno *some, a few*

It agrees adjectivally, but drops the **o** before a masculine singular noun:

Ha vendido **algunos** periódicos	*He has sold some newspapers*
La carta llegará **algún** día	*The letter will arrive some day*
Algunas de las lechugas son frescas	*Some of the lettuces are fresh*

d Unlike English, none of the above may be used after a negative. The appropriate negative is used instead:

No pueden ofrecer **nada**   *They cannot offer anything*
(see Chapter 12)

11.2 Mucho, poco, tanto, todo

These agree when used as adjectives or pronouns, but are invariable as adverbs:

a Mucho *much, many*; **poco** *little, few*

Corremos **mucho**	*We run a lot*
Construye **muchos** puentes	*He builds many bridges*
Duerme **poco**	*He sleeps little*
Plantan **pocos** pinos	*They are planting few pine trees*

b Tanto *so much, so many* (see also 9.3c)

Hay **tanta** mugre en el suelo	*There is so much dirt on the ground*
Las sandías tienen **tantas** pepitas	*Watermelons have so many pips*
Bebe **tanto**	*He drinks so much*

c Todo *all, every, whole*

Todo está listo	*Everything is ready*
Todos se acostaron temprano	*Everyone went to bed early*

As an adjective it must always be accompanied by the definite article, a demonstrative or possessive adjective, or an object pronoun:

Ha estado aquí **toda la** semana	*He has been here all week*
Todas las actrices son célebres	*All the actresses are famous*
Voy a revelar **todas mis** fotos	*I am going to get all my photos developed*
Hemos recibido **todo lo** que pedimos (see also 10.7f)	*We have received all we ordered*
Todos los que están en el rincón son tuyos	*All the ones in the corner are yours*
¿**Lo** apuntaste **todo**?	*Did you jot it all down?*

except:

when it means *each, every, any* in the singular:

Todo pasajero que lleva pasaporte español puede pasar por aquí	*Any passenger with a Spanish passport can go through this way*

or in the following expressions:

a/por todas partes	*everywhere*	de todos modos	*anyway*
a todos lados	*on all sides*		

del todo translates *completely*:

Está **del todo** lleno	*It is completely full*

todo el mundo (*everybody*) takes a singular verb:

Todo el mundo **está** feliz	*Everybody is happy*

11.3 Further indefinite adjectives and pronouns

a Varios(as) *several, various*

Encendieron **varias** luces	*They switched on several lights*
Varios de los plátanos están maduros	*Several of the bananas are ripe*
Hay **varias** palabras aquí que no entiende	*There are various words here he does not understand*

b Cualquiera *some, any* (vague)

It may drop the **a** before a noun:

Podría llegar a **cualquier** hora	*He could arrive at any time*
Puedes llevar **cualquiera** de los discos	*You can take any record you like*

c Los(las) demás *the others, the remainder; the other, the remaining*
Lo demás *the rest* (not referring to a specific noun)

Leí **los demás** capítulos de mi novela	*I read the remaining chapters in my novel*
Algunas de las chicas están en el comedor, pero no sabemos dónde están **las demás**	*Some of the girls are in the dining room, but we do not know where the rest are*
Esta parte es fácil, **lo demás** es bastante difícil	*This part is easy, the rest is quite difficult*

d Otro *other, another (one(s))*

It is never preceded by an indefinite article:

estas camisas y **las otras**	*these shirts and the other ones*
Están cargando **otra** camioneta	*They are loading up another van*
Este **otro** cristal está roto también	*This other pane is broken too*

e Tal(es) *such, such a*

No indefinite article may be used after **tal**:

No escribirá **tal** cosa	*He will not write such a thing*
Tales ejercicios son muy difíciles	*Such exercises are very difficult*

f Cada (invariable) *each, every*

As a pronoun it must be followed by **uno(a)**:

¿Cuánto cuesta **cada uno**?	*How much are they each?*
Cada avenida parece igual	*Each avenue seems the same*
¿Diste una propina a **cada** hombre?	*Did you give a tip to each man?*

g **La mayoría de** *most of* (individual units)
La mayor parte de *most of* (a single unit)

La mayoría de los estudiantes lo comprenden	*Most of the students understand it*
Se celebró **la mayor parte de** la fiesta al aire libre	*Most of the party was held in the open air*

h **Cierto** *certain, a certain* (before the noun); *definite* (after the noun)

In the first meaning it is never preceded by an indefinite article:

Ciertos funcionarios le aconsejaron que volviese al día siguiente	*Certain officials advised him to return the following day*
Cierto vecino avisó a la policía	*A certain neighbour notified the police*
Ha sido un éxito **cierto**	*It has been a definite success*

i **Mismo** *same* (before a noun); *-self*, etc. (after a noun, or pronoun)

As is translated by **que**:

Siempre hace la **misma** pregunta	*He always asks the same question*
Estos colores son los **mismos** que los otros	*These colours are the same as the others*
No podemos prometer lo **mismo**	*We cannot promise the same*
Maribel **misma** lo bordará	*Maribel will embroider it herself*
Lo tienes que conducir tú **mismo**	*You must drive it yourself*

note:
Mismo is also used after adverbs of time and place for emphasis:

Dejó el cuchillo aquí **mismo**	*She left the knife right here*
Va a reparar la radio ahora **mismo**	*He is going to repair the radio right now*

j **Ambos(as); los(las) dos** *both*

The second expression is used more frequently in everyday Spanish:

Ambas (**las dos**) azafatas son guapas	*Both air hostesses are pretty*
Se acordó de **ambos** (**los dos**) cuadros	*He remembered both pictures*

11.4 Linkage of indefinite adjectives and pronouns to an infinitive by 'que'

Tienes **alguna** ropa **que** lavar	*You have some clothes to be washed*
Encontró **algo que** comentar	*He found something to discuss*
No había **mucho que** organizar	*There was not much to be organised*
Tengo **cierta** idea **que** proponerte	*I have a certain idea to put to you*

12 Negatives

12.1 Simple negatives

A statement may be made negative by adding **no** between the subject and the verb:

La puerta es azul
The door is blue

La puerta **no** es azul
The door is not blue

No is placed between the subject and any object pronouns that precede the verb (10.3):

Yo se lo enviaré
I will send it to him

Yo **no** se lo enviaré
I will not send it to him

¿Vosotros los habeis escrito?
Have you written them?

¿Vosotros **no** los habéis escrito?
Haven't you written them?

In phrases like *not me, not today*, etc., the Spanish **no** usually comes after the word or phrase it qualifies:

yo **no**
hoy **no**
el que está allí **no**, el otro

not me
not today
not the one that is over there, the other one

When *not* forms a kind of object of verbs of saying, hoping, thinking, etc., it is translated by **que no**:

Esperas **que no**
Dijo **que no**
Creemos **que no**
Supongo **que no**

You hope not
He said not
We don't think so/We think not
I suppose not

note also:

claro **que no**

of course not

The positive form is **que sí**:

Esperas **que sí**
claro **que sí**
Supongo **que sí**

You hope so
of course (yes)
I suppose so

See also section 16.29.

49

12.2 Double negatives

no ... nada	*nothing*	no ... tampoco	*not ... either*
no ... nadie	*nobody*	no ... ni ... ni	*neither ... nor*
no ... nunca	*never*	no ... ni siquiera	*not even*
no ... jamás	*never* (stronger)	no ... más	*no longer*
no ... ninguno	*no* (adjective)	no ... más que	*only*

a When any of the above appear after a verb they must be preceded by **no**:

Ellos **no** escogieron **nada**	*They did not choose anything*
No nieva **nunca** allí	*It never snows there*
No lo sabe ella **tampoco**	*She does not know either*
Eso **no** le interesa **más**	*That does not interest him any longer*
No nos quedan **más que** 100 pesos	*We have only 100 pesos left*

b **Ninguno** agrees, but drops the **o** in front of masculine singular nouns. It should not be used in the plural:

¿No oyes **ningún** pájaro?	*Can't you hear any birds?*
No va a llamar a **ninguno** de los clientes	*He is not going to call any of the clients*
No tenemos **ninguna** mañana libre esta semana	*We have no free morning this week*

c There are three degrees of negation:

No tiene dinero	*He has no money*
No tiene **ningún** dinero	*He hasn't any money*
No tiene dinero **alguno**	*He hasn't any money at all*

d **Nadie** and **ni ... ni** may be preceded by personal **a** (19.5c):

No espero **a nadie**	*I am not waiting for anyone*
No conocéis **ni a** Pablo **ni a** Esteban	*You don't know either Paul or Stephen*

e **Nada** means *not at all* when qualifying an adjective or adverb:

La estatua no es **nada** impresionante	*The statue is not at all impressive*

f **Nadie, nada** and **ninguno** are linked to an infinitive by **que**:

No tengo **nada que** leer	*I have nothing to read*
No había **nadie que** preguntar	*There was nobody to ask*
No tenía **ninguna** comida **que** preparar	*She had no meal to prepare*

g Jamás used after the verb but not preceded by **no** means *ever*:

¿**No** visita **jamás** a su tía?	*Does he never visit his aunt?*
¿Visita **jamás** a su tía?	*Does he ever visit his aunt?*

h Two negatives may be compounded as follows:

La vieja no ve **nunca** a **nadie** ahora	*The old woman never sees anyone now*
La tienda no vende **nunca nada** barato	*The shop never sells anything cheap*

i Two interdependent verbs may never be split by a negative:

No **ha conducido** nunca un coche	*He has never driven a car*
No **pueden recordar** nada	*They cannot remember anything*
No **está cenando** más	*He is no longer having supper*

12.3 Use of negatives before a verb

With the exception of **más** and **más que** the negatives above may be placed before the verb. **No** is no longer used with them. The adverbs **jamás, nunca, tampoco, ni siquiera** go in the same position as **no** in 12.2 above:

Nadie lo confirmó	*Nobody confirmed it*
Tú **nunca** olvidarás ese accidente	*You will never forget that accident*
Ni esta casa **ni** la otra está en venta	*Neither this house nor the other one is for sale*
Ninguna de las dependientas está enferma	*None of the shop assistants is ill*
Tampoco está limpia la mesa	*The table is not clean either*
Ni siquiera le gustaba el helado	*He didn't even like the ice cream*

Ni used on its own can also mean *not even, not a single*:

El **ni** había empezado a leer el libro	*He had not even begun to read his book*
No había **ni** un barco en el río	*There was not a single boat on the river*

12.4 Negatives in short replies

Practically all these negatives may be used without a verb in a short statement:

¿Quién está ausente? **Nadie.**	*Who is absent? Nobody.*
¿Cuántas veces has esquiado? **Nunca.**	*How many times have you skied? Never.*
¿Cuál de las dos lo hizo? **Ni** Rosa **ni** Nuria.	*Which of the two did it? Neither Rosa nor Nuria.*
El no está de acuerdo. Yo **tampoco.**	*He does not agree. Nor do I.*

(see also 16.29f)

12.5 Negatives in comparisons

The negatives must be used in the following type of comparison:

Estás jugando mejor que **nunca**	*You are playing better than ever*
Más que **nada** les gustaría vivir en el campo	*More than anything they would like to live in the country*
Tienen más dinero que **ninguno** de nuestros amigos	*They have more money than any of our friends*

12.6 Other negatives

a Todavía ... no *still ... not*; no ... todavía *not ... yet*

Todavía no se atreve a saltar	*He still does not dare jump*
No hemos devuelto la llave **todavía**	*We have not returned the key yet*
¿Se ha despertado? No, **todavía no.**	*Has he woken up? No, not yet.*

b Sin *without*

Salió **sin** su sombrero	*He went out without his hat*

Sin must be followed by a negative where English uses a positive adverb, etc.:

Regresaste **sin** haber comprado **nada**	*You returned without having bought anything*
Se fueron **sin** ver a **nadie**	*They left without seeing anyone*

As in 12.2c, there are three degrees of negation:

Lo haremos **sin** problema	*We will do it without any problem*
Lo haremos **sin ningún** problema	
Lo haremos **sin problema alguno**	*We will do it without the slightest problem*

c Sin que is used before a finite verb and takes the subjunctive (16.16c):

Lo empezaron **sin que** nos diésemos cuenta	*They began it without our realising it*

d Sino translates *but* after a negative where the first statement is clearly contradicted:

No busca el Ayuntamiento **sino** la comisaría	*He is not looking for the town hall but the police station*

No viajaremos en tren **sino** en avión   *We won't travel by train but by plane*
but

Yo no fumo, **pero** no me molesta   *I don't smoke, but I don't mind*
si Vd. quiere fumar   *if you want to smoke*

Sino can also mean *but* in the sense of *except*:

No te lo puede decir nadie   *Nobody can tell you but her*
sino ella

e Sino que is used before a finite verb:

El pueblo no sólo tiene un hotel de   *The town not only has a first class*
primera clase, **sino que** también   *hotel, but it also has some excellent*
tiene unos restaurantes excelentes   *restaurants*

f Further translations of *not at all* (12.2e):

Gracias. **De nada/No hay**   *Thank you. Not at all.*
de qué.
¡Estás disilusionado?   *Are you disappointed?*
En absoluto.   *Not at all.*

13 Interrogatives and exclamations

13.1 Interrogatives

a ¿Qué? ¿Cuál? *Which? What?*

In Spanish **qué** is used exclusively to translate *which* or *what* as an adjective:

¿**Qué** disco vas a comprar?	*Which record are you going to buy?*
¿**Qué** platos les gustan más?	*What dishes do they like most?*

As pronouns **qué** and **cuál** may be distinguished as follows:

Which is normally translated by **cuál(es)**:

¿**Cuál** de estas carreteras es la mejor?	*Which of these roads is the best?*
¿**Cuáles** de estos zapatos son los de él?	*Which of these shoes are his?*

What is normally translated by **qué**:

¿**Qué** os asustó?	*What frightened you?*
¿Con **qué** lo vamos a cubrir?	*What are we going to cover it with?*
¿**Qué** están sembrando?	*What are they sowing?*

But in the question *what is/are . . . ?*, **qué** aims to define an individual person or thing, etc. or a single class of them:

¿**Qué** es Rodrigo? Es futbolista.	*What is Rodrigo? He is a football player.*
¿**Qué** son los pulmones?	*What are lungs?*

Cuál asks for more specific information or tries to make a distinction between related people or objects, etc.:

¿**Cuál** es la capital de Colombia? Bogotá.	*What is the capital of Colombia? Bogotá.*
¿**Cuál** es su apellido?	*What is your surname?*
¿**Cuál** es la diferencia entre jerez y manzanilla?	*What is the difference between sherry and manzanilla?*
¿**Cuál** es su opinión?	*What is your opinion?*

b ¿Quién(es)?   *Who?* (subject or after preposition)
   ¿A quién(es)?   *Whom?* (object)
   ¿De quién(es)? *Whose?*

¿**Quién** estaba remando?	*Who was rowing?*
¿**Quién** asistió a la boda? ⎱	
¿**Quiénes** asistieron a la boda? ⎰	*Who attended the wedding?*
¿**A quién** detuvieron?	*Whom did they arrest?*
¿**A quién** lo prestarás?	*Whom will you lend it to?*
¿**De quién** es este reloj?	*Whose is this watch?*

¿**De quién?** may never be placed next to the noun like an adjective. **Cuyo** (10.7) may never be used in questions.

c ¿Cuándo?   *When?*
   ¿Dónde?   *Where?*
   ¿Adónde?   *Where . . . to?*
   ¿Cómo?   *How?*
   ¿Por qué? *Why?*
   ¿Cuánto?   *How much/many?* (it agrees when used adjectivally)

¿**Cuándo** ocurrió el terremoto?	*When did the earthquake happen?*
¿**Dónde** está la farmacia?	*Where is the chemist?*
¿**Adónde** vamos ahora?	*Where are we going (to) now?*
¿**Cómo** se puede quitar esta mancha?	*How can one remove this stain?*
¿**Por qué** no le operaron en seguida?	*Why didn't they operate on him immediately?*

¿**Cómo?** is also used in conversation when asking someone to repeat what they have just said:

– Su dirección es: Avenida Artigas 2036, primer piso, oficina no. 103
–¿**Cómo?**
His address is: Avenida Artigas 2036, first floor, office no. 103.
Sorry, could you say that again?

d All the above interrogatives are used in indirect questions as well:

No sabe **cuál** escogerá	*He does not know which he will choose*
El capitán se preguntó **por qué** habían perdido	*The captain wondered why they had lost*
Los detectives están investigando **cómo** entraron los ladrones	*The detectives are investigating how the thieves got in*

13.2 Exclamations

a Quién, cuánto, cómo and qué may also be used in exclamations:

¡Quién lo hubiera creído!	*Who would have believed it!*
¡Cuánto pesa!	*How heavy it is!*
¡Cómo! ¿Ha subido otra vez el precio del pan?	*What! Has the price of bread gone up yet again?*

b Qué in this context translates:

i *what, what a* + noun

The indefinite article is never translated. If, as is usually the case, the adjective follows the noun, it is linked to it by **más** or **tan**:

¡Qué lástima!	*What a pity!*
¡Qué perro **tan/más** feroz!	*What a fierce dog!*
¡Qué calcetines **tan/más** sucios!	*What dirty socks!*

ii *how* + adjective or adverb:

¡Qué ridículo!	*How ridiculous!*
¡Qué raro!	*How strange!*

14 Numerals, time and measurement

14.1 Cardinal numbers

0	cero	19	diez y nueve	90	noventa
1	uno, una		diecinueve	100	ciento
2	dos	20	veinte	101	ciento uno(a)
3	tres	21	veintiuno(a)	150	ciento cincuenta
4	cuatro	22	veintidós	200	doscientos(as)
5	cinco	23	veintitrés	300	trescientos(as)
6	seis	24	veinticuatro	400	cuatrocientos(as)
7	siete	25	veinticinco	500	quinientos(as)
8	ocho	26	veintiséis	600	seiscientos(as)
9	nueve	27	veintisiete	700	setecientos(as)
10	diez	28	veintiocho	800	ochocientos(as)
11	once	29	veintinueve	900	novecientos(as)
12	doce	30	treinta	1000	mil
13	trece	31	treinta y uno(a)	1120	mil ciento veinte
14	catorce	32	treinta y dos	2000	dos mil
15	quince	40	cuarenta	10.000	diez mil
16	diez y seis	50	cincuenta	100.000	cien mil
	dieciséis	60	sesenta	1.000.000	un millón
17	diez y siete	70	setenta	2.000.000	dos millones
	diecisiete	80	ochenta	1.000.000.000.000	un billón
18	diez y ocho				
	dieciocho				

notes:

uno drops the **o** before masculine nouns, including in compound numerals: **un** día, veinti**ún** libros.

1, 21, 31, etc. and 200, 300, 400, etc. have feminine forms: veinti**una** casas, doscient**as** veinte pesetas.

ciento is used before numbers smaller than 100, **cien** is used at all other times: **ciento** veinte, *but* **cien** pájaros, **cien** mil.

y (*and*) occurs only between tens and ones: *36* treinta **y** seis, *but 160* ciento sesenta, *204* doscientos cuatro. **Y** changes to **i**, when 16–19 are written as one word and in the twenties.

millón and **billón** take **de** before a noun: un millón **de** naranjas, dos billones **de** dólares.

mil and **cien** are never preceded by an article: **mil** veces, **cien** árboles. **Mil** only occurs in the plural when meaning *thousands of*: **miles** de insectos, *but* seis **mil**.

The cardinals tend to precede the ordinals:

las **dos** primeras filas	*the first two rows*
los **tres** últimos vagones	*the last two carriages*

The digits of telephone numbers may be read out individually, but are frequently broken up into groups of two:

221.99.06 (el) dos – veintiuno – noventa y nueve – cero seis

14.2 Ordinal numbers

first	primero (primer)	*sixth*	sexto
second	segundo	*seventh*	séptimo
third	tercero (tercer)	*eighth*	octavo
fourth	cuarto	*ninth*	noveno
fifth	quinto	*tenth*	décimo

These numerals agree adjectivally and normally precede the noun they qualify, except in royal titles. **Primero** and **tercero** drop the **o** before a masculine singular noun:

el **tercer** mes	*the third month*
la **séptima** edición	*the seventh edition*
Carlos **cuarto**	*Charles IV* (note absence of definite article)
Isabel **segunda**	*Elizabeth II*

Beyond **décimo** they are rarely used as they become extremely complex. They are replaced by the cardinal numbers, which are normally placed after the noun:

el siglo **veinte**	*the twentieth century*
Alfonso **trece**	*Alfonso XIII*

They are most commonly abbreviated by adding º or ª to the number, depending on the gender of the noun they qualify:

1ª clase	*1st class*
2º piso	*2nd floor*

14.3 Collective numerals

All of these are followed by **de** + noun.

2	un par	*100*	un centenar, una centena
10	una decena	*100s*	cientos/centenares
12	una docena	*1000*	un millar
20	una veintena	*1000s*	miles/millares
30	una treintena*		

* All of the major numerals from 30 to 90 can be converted in this way.

14.4 Fractions and percentages

a Simple fractions

$\frac{1}{2}$	un medio*	$\frac{2}{3}$	dos tercios
$\frac{1}{3}$	un tercio	$\frac{1}{4}$	un cuarto

* *half:*
   (noun) la mitad: la mitad de la torta   *half the cake*
   (adjective) medio: media hora   *half an hour*
   (adverb) medio (invariable):
           Estaban medio dormidos   *They were half asleep*

note also:

   un kilo y medio   1$\frac{1}{2}$ *kilos*;   dos horas y media   2$\frac{1}{2}$ *hours*

b Percentages

por ciento, por cien   *per cent*

Both are generally preceded by an article:

El treinta por ciento del país   *Thirty per cent of the country*
   es árido   *is arid*
La población ha aumentado en   *The population has increased*
   un 5%   *by 5%*

14.5 Arithmetical signs

+	más, y	$4 + 6 = 10$	cuatro más/y seis son diez
−	menos	$10 - 7 = 3$	diez menos siete son tres
×	por	$5 \times 5 = 25$	cinco por cinco son veinticinco
÷	dividido por	$12 \div 6 = 2$	doce dividido por seis son dos

14.6 Time

a General expressions of *time*

¿Qué hora es? ⎫	*What is the time?*
¿Qué horas son? ⎭	
Es la una	*It is one o'clock*
Son las dos	*It is two o'clock*
(from 2 o'clock onwards the expression is in the plural)	
¿A qué hora?	*At what time?*
A la una	*At one*
A las tres	*At three*

Time past the hour:

la una y diez	*1.10*
las cinco y cuarto	*5.15*
las ocho y media	*8.30*

Time before the hour:

las diez menos veinte	*9.40*
las doce menos cuarto	*11.45*

In Latin America the following expression is frequently used:

Faltan veinte minutos para las diez	*It is 9.40*
Falta un cuarto para las doce	*It is 11.45*

When referring to a timetable, time may be expressed as follows:

a las siete cincuenta y tres	*at 7.53*
a las catorce cero ocho	*at 14.08*
a las veintidós treinta	*at 22.30*

mediodía *midday*   medianoche *midnight*
These are not combined, as they are in French, with minutes before or after twelve.

la madrugada	*the morning (before dawn)*
la mañana	*the morning (later, or in general)*
la tarde	*the afternoon and evening*
la noche	*the night*
de la madrugada	*a.m. (before dawn)*
de la mañana	*a.m. (any time in the morning)*
de la tarde	*p.m. (before 7 or 8)*
de la noche	*p.m. (7 or 8 to 12 or 2 a.m.)*

examples:

a las cinco de la madrugada	*at 5 a.m.*
Son las ocho de la mañana	*It is 8 a.m.*
Son las siete de la tarde	*It is 7 p.m.*
Son las once de la noche	*It is 11 p.m.*
por la mañana	*in the morning*
por la tarde	*in the afternoon or evening*
por la noche	*in the night*

la mañana, etc., may be combined as follows:

mañana por la mañana	*tomorrow morning*
ayer por la tarde	*yesterday afternoon*
el lunes por la noche	*on Monday night*
por la mañana temprano	*early in the morning*

but:

anoche	*last night*
esta mañana/tarde/noche	*this morning/afternoon/tonight*
muy de madrugada	*very early in the morning*
de día/noche	*by day/night*
anteayer	*the day before yesterday*
hoy	*today*
pasado mañana	*the day after tomorrow*
a las cuatro en punto	*at exactly 4 o'clock*
a las seis y pico a un poco más de las seis }	*just after six*
sobre/a eso de/hacia las diez	*at around ten*
de nueve a una desde las nueve hasta la una }	*from nine to one*
un cuarto de hora	*a quarter of an hour*
tres cuartos de hora	*three quarters of an hour*
media hora	*half an hour*
dos veces por hora	*twice an hour*

b The days of the week

For Spaniards and Latin Americans the week begins on Monday. The days are all masculine:

lunes	*Monday*	jueves	*Thursday*	sábado	*Saturday*
martes	*Tuesday*	viernes	*Friday*	domingo	*Sunday*
miércoles	*Wednesday*				

el lunes	*on Monday*
los martes	*on Tuesdays*
los sábados	*on Saturdays*

(only **sábado** and **domingo** have separate plural forms)

Mañana es viernes	Tomorrow is Friday
el fin de semana	the weekend
quince días	a fortnight
de hoy en ocho días	today week
de hoy en quince días	today fortnight

c Months

All months are masculine:

enero	January	mayo	May	septiembre	September
febrero	February	junio	June	octubre	October
marzo	March	julio	July	noviembre	November
abril	April	agosto	August	diciembre	December

d Dates

el primero de junio	the first of June
el dos de diciembre	the second of December

note:

The use of the cardinal number is compulsory from the second onwards, but optional for the first. *The first of June* may therefore also be translated as **el uno de junio**.

Día (*day*) may also be inserted in the above expressions, hence:

el **día** dos de diciembre

Sábado, el tres de mayo	Saturday, 3rd May
el treinta de abril de mil novecientos ochenta y dos	30.4.1982

note:

Nineteen hundred must be translated as *thousand nine hundred*.
De is inserted before both the month and the year.
El is usually omitted in letter headings.

¿Qué fecha es hoy? Es el ocho de mayo. ⎫	What is the date today?
¿A cuántos estamos? Estamos a ocho de mayo. ⎭	It is 8th May.
en 1975	in 1975
los años ochenta	the eighties
10 antes de Jesucristo (10 a. de J.C.)	10 BC
50 después de Jesucristo (50 A.C./D.C.)	AD 50

e Seasons

la primavera	spring	el otoño	autumn
el verano	summer	el invierno	winter

en (la) primavera   *in spring*

Miscellaneous expressions

el lunes (mes, año) pasado	*last Monday (month, year)*
la semana pasada	*last week*
en diciembre pasado	*last December*
el último mes	*the last month (of a series)*
la última semana	*the last week (of a series)*
al día siguiente	*the next (following) day*
a la mañana siguiente	*the next (following) morning*
la semana próxima/entrante/que viene	*next (this coming) week*
el próximo lunes el lunes que viene }	*next Monday*
el próximo mes de mayo el mayo que viene }	*next May*
el mes (año) entrante/que viene	*next month (year)*
a primera(s) hora(s) de la mañana	*in the early hours of the morning*
al principio del día	*at the beginning of the day*
al principio de la semana	*at the beginning of the week*
al principio del otoño	*at the beginning of the autumn*
a principios de mes (abril, año)	*at the beginning of the month (April, the year)*
a media mañana	*in the middle of the morning*
a mediados de mes (abril, año)	*in the middle of the month (April, the year)*
en pleno verano	*in the middle of the summer*
en plena primavera	*in the middle of spring*
al final de la tarde	*at the end of the afternoon*
al fin/final del día	*at the end of the day*
a finales de mes (marzo, año)	*at (around) the end of the month (March, the year)*
cada día, semana, etc. todos los días, todas las semanas }	*every day, week, etc.*
dos veces al/por día (mes, año)	*twice a day (month, year)*
dos veces a la/por semana	*twice a week*

14.7 Translation of *time*

Time in general: **tiempo**

No tengo **tiempo** ahora	*I haven't got any time now*
Duró poco **tiempo**	*It lasted a short time*

Time of the clock: **hora**

¿Qué **hora** es?	*What is the time?*
¿Tiene Vd. **hora**?	*Have you got the time?*
Es **hora** de comer	*It is time to eat*

One or more occasions: **vez**

tres **veces**	*three times*
a **veces**/algunas **veces**	*sometimes*
de **vez** en cuando	*from time to time*
esta **vez**	*this time*

A short period of time: **un rato**

Sólo tuvimos que esperar **un rato**	*We only had to wait a short time*

A long time: **mucho tiempo**

hace **mucho tiempo**	*a long time ago*
No tardará **mucho tiempo**	*It won't be a long time*

Historical period: **época**

en aquella **época**	*at that time*
en nuestra **época**	*in our time*

Specific moment: **momento**

en este **momento**	*at this time*

14.8 Age

¿Cuántos años tiene?	
¿Qué edad tiene?	*How old is he?*
Tiene 18 (años)	*He is 18*
Tiene unos 30 años	*He is around 30*
Tiene cinco años y pico	*He is just over five*
Me lleva 7 años	
Es 7 años mayor que yo	*He is 7 years older than me*
a los 25 años	*at the age of 25*
No llega a 40 años	*He is not quite 40*
Va a cumplir diez años en marzo	*He will be ten in March*
Acaba de cumplir 70 años	*He has just turned 70*

14.9 Measurement

¿Qué longitud tiene ...? *or* ¿Cuánto tiene/es de largo...?		*How long is ...?*
altura	alto	*high*
espesor	espeso ⎫ grueso ⎭	*thick*
profundidad	profundo ⎫ hondo ⎭	*deep*
anchura	ancho	*wide*

Tiene 10 metros de largo/longitud		*It is 10 metres long*
	alto/altura	*high*
	espeso/espesor grueso/ ⎫⎭	*thick*
	profundo/profundidad hondo ⎫⎭	*deep*
	ancho/anchura	*wide*

(In each of the above cases the adjective is invariable.)

La altura del edificio es de 50 m	*The height of the building is 50 m*
La caja es igual de alta que de ancha	*The box is as high as it is wide*
¿Qué mide Vd.? Mido 1,60 m	*How tall are you? I am 1.60 m tall*
¿Qué mide el paquete?	*What are the measurements of the parcel?*
La longitud del corredor pasa de 10 m ⎫ El corredor tiene más de 10 m de largo ⎭	*The corridor is more than 10 m long*
Le lleva 3 cm a su padre	*He is 3 cm taller than his father*
Tu coche es 15 cm más ancho que el mío	*Your car is 15 cm wider than mine*
¿Cuánto pesa el sobre? Pesa 20 gramos	*How heavy is the letter? It weighs 20 grammes*

14.10 Distance

¿Qué distancia hay de aquí a Ayacucho?	*How far is it to Ayacucho from here?*
De aquí a Ayacucho hay 400 km	*Ayacucho is 400 km away*
¿Cuántos kilómetros hay de Lima a Ayacucho?	*How far is it from Lima to Ayacucho?*
¿A qué distancia queda Bellver?	*How far away is Bellver?*
Queda a unos 30 km de aquí	*It is around 30 km from here*
El castillo está a 2 km de la carretera	*The castle is 2 km off the main road*

15 Diminutive, augmentative and pejorative suffixes

Diminutive suffixes are used mainly to make something smaller or to show affection or occasionally distaste.

Augmentative suffixes are used mainly to make something larger, but often clumsier or uglier.

Pejorative suffixes are used to make something more unpleasant.

The diminutives are the most frequently encountered group.

The commonest suffixes in each category are included below. They are attached to the stem of the original word, i.e. after any final vowel has been removed. Sometimes further changes take place. Such words should therefore be recognised rather than invented by students of Spanish.

a Diminutives

-ito(ita)

un poco	*a little*	un poquito	*a very small amount*
un viejo	*an old man*	un viejecito	*a little old man*
casa	*house*	casita	*cottage*
bajo	*short (people)*	bajito	*very short (people)*
un rato	*a short while*	un ratito	*a very short while*

-illo(illa)

chico	*small boy*	chiquillo	*very small boy*
palo	*stick*	palillo	*small stick, toothpick*
campana	*bell*	campanilla	*small bell*

b Augmentatives

-ón(ona)

hombre	*man*	hombretón	*hefty great man*
puerta	*door*	portón	*large door*

-azo(aza)

gripe	*flu*	gripazo	*really bad bout of flu*
perro	*dog*	perrazo	*brute of a dog*

this suffix can also mean *a blow with*:

puño	*fist*	puñetazo	*punch*

-ote(ota)

grande	*large*	grandote	*huge*
palabra	*word*	palabrota	*swear word*

c Pejoratives

-ucho(ucha)

cuarto	*room*	cuartucho	*poky little room*
blanco	*white*	blancucho	*off white*

-acho(acha)

rico	*rich*	ricacho	*filthy rich*

-uzo (uza)

gente	*people*	gentuza	*scum*

-uco (uca)

ventana	*window*	ventanuca	*miserable little window*

-(z)uelo (a)

autor	*author*	autorzuelo	*hack*
gordo	*fat*	gordezuelo	*small and chubby*

16 Verbs

16.1 Introduction

All regular verbs in Spanish are divided into three conjugations, or groups, according to their endings in the infinitive:

-AR	-ER	-IR
hablar *to speak*	comer *to eat*	vivir *to live*

These three verbs have been used throughout the regular verb section to illustrate the formation of the Spanish tenses, with the exception of the adjectival present participle (16.25) and reflexive verbs (16.27). The English tenses have been illustrated by the first person singular or other relevant part of the verb *to speak*.

stem:

Unless otherwise stated, this means the infinitive less the final **-ar**, **-er** or **-ir**.

personal endings:

The order in which these are shown is as follows:

yo	*I*	(1st person singular)
tú	*you*	(2nd person singular)
él, ella, usted	*he, she, it, you*	(3rd person singular)
nosotros	*we*	(1st person plural)
vosotros	*you*	(2nd person plural)
ellos, ellas, ustedes	*they, you*	(3rd person plural)

(The different translations of *you* are explained in 4.1.)

Indicative tenses (16.2–16.11)

16.2 Present

a **English**

I speak, I do speak, I don't speak, do I speak?

b Formation

stem + present endings:

hablo	como	vivo
hablas	comes	vives
habla	come	vive
hablamos	comemos	vivimos
habláis	coméis	vivís
hablan	comen	viven

c Usage

As in English:

¿**Viven** en Madrid? — *Do they live in Madrid?*
Creo que **está** enfermo — *I think he is ill*
No **desayuna** a las ocho — *He does not have breakfast at eight*
Ella **trabaja** en una tienda — *She works in a shop*

and in addition:

i to convey an immediate or planned future:

Ya **voy** — *I am coming*
Le **escribimos** mañana — *We will write to him tomorrow*

ii as a softened command:

¿Me **traes** la mantequilla, por favor? — *Could you fetch me the butter, please?*

iii to translate *shall* in suggestions:

¿**Cierro** la puerta? — *Shall I shut the door?*
¿Nos **sentamos** aquí? — *Shall we sit down here?*

iv as a historic present – to convey actions more vividly in a narrative:

En 1881 **nace** Picasso en Málaga — *In 1881 Picasso was born in Málaga*

v to describe an action or state begun in the past and continuing into the present:

Está en casa desde las tres — *He has been at home since three*

(This is explained more fully in 18.11.)

vi The English form *I do speak* is often used for emphasis. This can be conveyed in Spanish by putting **sí** before the verb:

No habla francés, pero **sí** habla español — *He doesn't speak French, but he does speak Spanish*

16.3 Imperfect

a English

I was speaking, I used to speak

b Formation

Stem + imperfect endings:

hablaba	comía	vivía
hablabas	comías	vivías
hablaba	comía	vivía
hablábamos	comíamos	vivíamos
hablabais	comíais	vivíais
hablaban	comían	vivían

c Usage

Both English forms are translated by the Spanish imperfect, though the first may also be translated by the imperfect continuous (16.21) if there is a desire to emphasise the fact that an action was going on at a precise moment in the past, as in the second example below.

El sol **brillaba** y el cielo **era** de un azul claro
The sun was shining and the sky was bright blue

Cuando entré, mi hermana **estaba mirando** la televisión
When I went in, my sister was watching the television

En verano se **levantaba** muy temprano cada día
In the summer he used to get up early every day

The Spanish imperfect is also used to translate the English simple past (*I spoke*, etc.) in the following cases:

i   to describe habitual actions:

Se **ponía** nerviosa cada vez que **viajaba** en avión
She would get nervous every time she travelled by plane

ii   to describe settings or situations in the past:

Cuando los gemelos **tenían** 16 años, su padre murió
When the twins were 16, their father died

Hacía calor aquella tarde
It was hot that afternoon

including time:

Eran las cinco
It was five o'clock

iii generally when using verbs like those of wanting, thinking, knowing, fearing, being able, etc., conveying mental activity or a state of mind in the past:

> **Quería** saber dónde está el cine
> *He wanted to know where the cinema is*
>
> **Creíamos** que era un vino chileno
> *We thought it was a Chilean wine*
>
> ¿No **sabías** que se había ahogado?
> *Didn't you know he had drowned?*

16.4 Future

a English

I shall speak, I will speak

b Formation

Future stem (which in the case of regular verbs is the infinitive, but which in all cases ends in **-r**) + future endings – these, with the exception of the 2nd person plural, have the same sound as the present indicative of **haber**. The stress is always on the ending:

hablar**é**	comer**é**	vivir**é**
hablar**ás**	comer**ás**	vivir**ás**
hablar**á**	comer**á**	vivir**á**
hablar**emos**	comer**emos**	vivir**emos**
hablar**éis**	comer**éis**	vivir**éis**
hablar**án**	comer**án**	vivir**án**

c Usage

i   To convey a very definite future:

Estoy seguro que el avión **llegará** a tiempo	*I am sure the plane will arrive on time*
Les **veremos** mañana	*We will see them tomorrow*
Venceremos	*We shall overcome*

A weaker or more immediate future is conveyed by the present (16.2c):

Nos **encontramos** en el bar, entonces	*We'll meet at the bar then*

(See also (iv) below.)

ii For legal obligations:

Vd. **trabajará** de 8 a 1 y de 3 a 6   *You will work from 8 to 1 and from 3 to 6*

No **matarás**   *Thou shalt not kill*

iii To express possibility, supposition or surprise:

¿Qué **estará haciendo** ahora?   *What can he be doing now?*

¿**Estará** lista ya?   *Do you think she is ready yet?*

¿Qué **querrá** decir esto?   *What on earth does this mean?*

iv When *shall/will/shan't/won't* expresses a desire or polite request, it is translated by the present tense of **querer** + infinitive:

No **quiere** esforzarse   *He won't make any effort*

¿**Quieres** esperar un momento, por favor?   *Will you wait a minute, please?*

shall in suggestions is translated by the present:

¿**Comemos** ahora?   *Shall we eat now?*

v *I am going to*, etc. is frequently translated by the present tense of **ir a** + infinitive in Spanish:

Vamos a cenar en un restaurante   *We are going to have supper in a restaurant*

Also note the past form:

Iban a escuchar la radio   *They were going to listen to the radio*

16.5 Conditional

a English

I would speak, etc. (or: *I should . . .*, unless this implies obligation – see 18.4)

b Formation

Future stem + **-er/ir** imperfect endings:

hablaría	comería	viviría
hablarías	comerías	vivirías
hablaría	comería	viviría
hablaríamos	comeríamos	viviríamos
hablaríais	comeríais	viviríais
hablarían	comerían	vivirían

c Usage

Basically the same as in English:

El **compraría** un yate si tuviera dinero
He would buy a yacht if he had the money

Ella dijo que no **necesitaría** la máquina de escribir
She said she would not need the typewriter

Nos **gustaría** descansar
We would like to rest

The Spanish conditional may also be used to convey possibility, supposition and surprise when referring to events in the past:

Serían las diez cuando empezó a nevar
It must have been ten o'clock when it began to snow

but note:

i When the English *would* conveys a habit in the past, the imperfect is used:

Cuando estaban de vacaciones *When they were on holiday they*
comían fuera cada día   *would eat out every day*

ii The expression *would you like (to)* is translated by the present tense of **querer** when no condition is inferred:

¿**Quieres** tomar una copa? *Would you like a drink?*

iii *Would* indicating willingness in the past is translated by the imperfect or preterite of **querer** (or similar verb):

No **quería** esperar   *He would not wait*

16.6 Perfect

a English

I have spoken

b Formation

The present tense of **haber** + past participle:

he hablado	he comido	he vivido
has hablado	has comido	has vivido
ha hablado	ha comido	ha vivido
hemos hablado	hemos comido	hemos vivido
habéis hablado	habéis comido	habéis vivido
han hablado	han comido	han vivido

c Usage

Basically the same as in English:

Paco **ha telefoneado** a su amigo
Paco has phoned his friend

La enfermera todavía no le **ha dado** su medicina
The nurse still hasn't given him his medicine

but the present is used in the following cases:

i   where the English perfect is used to describe an action in the past and
continuing into the present:

Desde que **vive** en Suiza, se **siente** mucho mejor
Since he has been living in Switzerland, he has been feeling much better

This point is explained more fully in 18.11.

ii   the English expression *to have just (done something)*, which is rendered by
acabar de + infinitive:

Ella **acaba de salir**
She has just gone out

note:

Haber may never be separated from the past participle in compound tenses:

¿Se **ha duchado** Vd. hoy?
Have you had a shower today?

No lo **han probado** todavía
They haven't tasted it yet

16.7 Preterite (Simple past)

a English

I spoke, I did not speak, did I speak?

b Formation

Stem + preterite endings:

habl**é**	com**í**	viv**í**
habl**aste**	com**iste**	viv**iste**
habl**ó**	com**ió**	viv**ió**
habl**amos**	com**imos**	viv**imos**
habl**asteis**	com**isteis**	viv**isteis**
habl**aron**	com**ieron**	viv**ieron**

c Usage

In both written and spoken Spanish to describe completed actions or events in the past:

Se **levantó**, se **lavó** y se **afeitó**   *He got up, washed and shaved*
La guerra civil española **empezó**   *The Spanish Civil War began in 1936*
en 1936

Where the English simple past is used to describe settings or repeated actions in the past, the imperfect is used (see 16.3c):

Salían juntos todos los sábados   *They went out together every Saturday*
No **tenía** ese coche la última   *He did not have that car the last time*
vez que le vimos   *we saw him*

The imperfect is also used in most cases where verbs of wanting, thinking, knowing, fearing, etc. are being used in the past (16.3c). Sometimes these verbs have a different meaning in the preterite:

supe   *I found out*
conocí   *I met, got to know* (people, etc.)
pude   *I succeeded in*
quise   *I intended*
no quise   *I refused*

The translation of the English simple past in conditions is covered in 16.19.

16.8 Pluperfect

a English

I had spoken

b Formation

Imperfect of **haber** + past participle:

había hablado	había comido	había vivido
habías hablado	habías comido	habías vivido
había hablado	había comido	había vivido
habíamos hablado	habíamos comido	habíamos vivido
habíais hablado	habíais comido	habíais vivido
habían hablado	habían comido	habían vivido

c Usage

On the whole the same as in English:

Habían comprado medio kilo de bombones
They had bought half a kilo of sweets

Nos dijo donde **había encontrado** la carta
He told us where he had found the letter

but the imperfect is used:

i   when the English pluperfect describes an action begun in the past and continuing into another action:

Trabajaba desde hace dos años como actriz cuando la conociste
She had been working as an actress for two years when you met her

See 18.11 for other examples.

ii in the expression **acabar de** + infinitive to translate *I had just done something,* etc.:

Cuando le llamé, **acababa de hablar** con el jefe
When I called him, he had just spoken to the boss

16.9 Past anterior

a English

I had spoken

b Formation

Preterite of **haber** + past participle:

hube hablado	hube comido	hube vivido
hubiste hablado	hubiste comido	hubiste vivido
hubo hablado	hubo comido	hubo vivido
hubimos hablado	hubimos comido	hubimos vivido
hubisteis hablado	hubisteis comido	hubisteis vivido
hubieron hablado	hubieron comido	hubieron vivido

c Usage

It is occasionally used in time clauses in literary Spanish instead of the pluperfect where this tense is contrasted with the preterite:

Apenas se **hubieron sentado**, cuando el ministro anunció su programa
They had scarcely sat down when the minister announced his programme

16.10 Future perfect

a English

I will/shall have spoken

b Formation

Future of **haber** + past participle:

habré hablado	habré comido	habré vivido
habrás hablado	habrás comido	habrás vivido
habrá hablado	habrá comido	habrá vivido
habremos hablado	habremos comido	habremos vivido
habréis hablado	habréis comido	habréis vivido
habrán hablado	habrán comido	habrán vivido

c Usage

As in English:

Habrá ido de vacaciones antes de que regresemos de Italia
He will have gone on holiday before we get back from Italy

It also indicates conjecture, normally when referring to things in the recent past:

Ya **habrá terminado** su trabajo
He must have finished his work by now

Les **habrá gustado** la película, ¿no?
They must have liked the film, mustn't they?

16.11 Conditional perfect

a English

I would have spoken

b Formation

Conditional of **haber** + past participle:

habría hablado	habría comido	habría vivido
habrías hablado	habrías comido	habrías vivido
habría hablado	habría comido	habría vivido
habríamos hablado	habríamos comido	habríamos vivido
habríais hablado	habríais comido	habríais vivido
habrían hablado	habrían comido	habrían vivido

c Usage

As in English:

El equipo **habría ganado**, si hubiera jugado mejor
The team would have won if they had played better

Creía que ella lo **habría mandado** por avión
He thought she would have sent it by airmail

16.12 The subjunctive

This is a mood, or set of tenses, which has virtually disappeared from English, but which is still much used in both written and spoken Spanish. In English the subjunctive has largely been replaced by the indicative, but it can still be seen at work in certain phrases, although some of these forms now seem rather archaic. Perhaps the clearest illustration of the English subjunctive at work is the verb *to be*:

> *If he be found guilty* . . . .⎫
> *Praise be to God*   ⎬   present
> *If I were you,* . . . . . .   past

It is also conveyed by certain auxiliaries such as *may, might, were to, should.*

The subjunctive exists in Spanish to cover possible, hypothetical, or as yet unrealised situations, to express doubt, emotion, the desire to influence events or another person's actions, and in a number of other cases, all of which are covered in greater detail in 16.14–16.20.

16.13 Formation of the subjunctive

a Present

For all forms other than the 1st person singular, take the 1st person singular present indicative and remove the final **o**. The **-ar** verbs then add the present indicative endings of the **-er** verbs, and the **-er** and **-ir** verbs add the present indicative endings of the **-ar** verbs.

The 1st and 3rd person singular of the present subjunctive are the same.

habl**e**	com**a**	viv**a**
habl**es**	com**as**	viv**as**
habl**e**	com**a**	viv**a**
habl**emos**	com**amos**	viv**amos**
habl**éis**	com**áis**	viv**áis**
habl**en**	com**an**	viv**an**

b Imperfect

Take the 3rd person plural of the preterite and remove **-ron**. Then add the imperfect subjunctive endings:

habla**se**	comie**se**	vivie**se**
habla**ses**	comie**ses**	vivie**ses**
habla**se**	comie**se**	vivie**se**
hablá**semos**	comié**semos**	vivié**semos**
habla**seis**	comie**seis**	vivie**seis**
habla**sen**	comie**sen**	vivie**sen**

c Conditional

Take the 3rd person plural of the preterite as above, remove **-ron**, and add the conditional subjunctive endings:

habla**ra**	comie**ra**	vivie**ra**
habla**ras**	comie**ras**	vivie**ras**
habla**ra**	comie**ra**	vivie**ra**
hablá**ramos**	comié**ramos**	vivié**ramos**
habla**rais**	comie**rais**	vivie**rais**
habla**ran**	comie**ran**	vivie**ran**

The main instance where the conditional subjunctive is not interchangeable with the imperfect subjunctive is when it is used in the main clause as an alternative for the conditional indicative of **poder**, **deber** and **querer**:

¿Me **pudiera** (*or* podría) mostrar el horario?
Could you show me the timetable?

Vd. **debiera** (*or* debería) reservar una habitación en el hotel
You should reserve a room at the hotel

Quisiera (*or* querría) probarme esa chaqueta gris
I would like to try on that grey jacket

d Perfect

Present subjunctive of **haber** + past participle:

haya hablado	haya comido	haya vivido
hayas hablado	hayas comido	hayas vivido
haya hablado	haya comido	haya vivido
hayamos hablado	hayamos comido	hayamos vivido
hayáis hablado	hayáis comido	hayáis vivido
hayan hablado	hayan comido	hayan vivido

e Pluperfect

Imperfect subjunctive of **haber** + past participle:

hubiese hablado	hubiese comido	hubiese vivido
hubieses hablado	hubieses comido	hubieses vivido
hubiese hablado	hubiese comido	hubiese vivido
hubiésemos hablado	hubiésemos comido	hubiésemos vivido
hubieseis hablado	hubieseis comido	hubieseis vivido
hubiesen hablado	hubiesen comido	hubiesen vivido

79

f Conditional perfect

Conditional subjunctive of **haber** + past participle:

hubiera hablado	hubiera comido	hubiera vivido
hubieras hablado	hubieras comido	hubieras vivido
hubiera hablado	hubiera comido	hubiera vivido
hubiéramos hablado	hubiéramos comido	hubiéramos vivido
hubierais hablado	hubierais comido	hubierais vivido
hubieran hablado	hubieran comido	hubieran vivido

The conditional perfect subjunctive is interchangeable with the pluperfect subjunctive except when it is used in the main clause as an alternative for the conditional perfect indicative:

Hubiéramos (*or* habríamos) **conseguido** el dinero ayer, pero el banco estaba cerrado
We would have got the money yesterday, but the bank was shut

16.14 Sequence of tenses

On the whole the subjunctive tends to be used in subordinate clauses. The tense of the subjunctive is largely governed by the tense of the verb in the main clause. The following is a guide:

main clause	**subordinate clause**
Present	
Imperative	
Future	Present
Perfect	Perfect
Future perfect	

main clause	**subordinate clause**
Imperfect	Imperfect
Conditional	Conditional
Preterite	
Pluperfect	Pluperfect
Conditional Perfect	Conditional Perfect

examples:

Dígale que **venga** (imperative + pres. subjunc.)
Tell him to come

Dudo que **haya ocurrido** (pres. indic. + perf. subjunc.)
I doubt that it has happened

Era improbable que lo **hubiese vendido** (imperf. indic. + pluperf. subjunc.)
It was unlikely that he had sold it

Esperaremos hasta que **termine** el concierto (future indic. + pres. subjunc.)
We will wait until the concert finishes

Les **pedí** que **subieran** al autobús (preterite indic. + pres. subjunc.)
I asked them to get into the bus

16.15 Main uses of the subjunctive

In the situations listed below the subjunctive is required in the dependent clause if the subject is different from that in the main clause. The dependent clause is in this case introduced by **que**. If the subject is the same in both cases, an infinitive may be used:

Quiero que me **compres** unas cebollas   *I want you to buy me some onions*

but:

Quiero **comprar** una maleta   *I want to buy a suitcase*

a After verbs of influence such as those expressing commands, wishes, requests, permission, prohibition, advice, etc.:

El médico le aconsejó que se **acostara** temprano   *The doctor advised him to go to bed early*
Dígale que lo **entregue** mañana   *Tell him to hand it in tomorrow*
Queremos que **traduzcan** el artículo al alemán   *We want them to translate the article into German*
Nos pidió que le **ayudáramos**   *He asked us to help him*

The following verbs may take an infinitive even if there is a change of subject: **hacer, mandar, dejar, permitir, aconsejar, ordenar, prohibir, consentir, rogar**:

Me permitieron que **aparcara** el coche aquí

or:

Me permitieron **aparcar** el coche aquí
They allowed me to park the car here

b After expressions of emotion or reaction: hope, regret, surprise, joy, fear, worry, etc.:

Siento que su madre **haya muerto**   *I am sorry your mother has died*
Le sorprende que no **hayan podido** reparar el reloj   *He is surprised that they have not been able to repair the watch*
Les dio mucho gusto saber que **hubieras tenido** tanto éxito   *They were very pleased to know you had been so successful*

In some of these expressions there is no dependent clause:

¡Ojalá **hiciera** sol!   *If only it were sunny!*
¡Qué **tengas** suerte!   *I wish you luck!*
¡Quién lo **hubiera adivinado**!   *Who would have guessed!*

The verbs **esperar** (*to hope*) and **temer** (*to fear*) may take the indicative or subjunctive:

Espero que se **hayan divertido**/se **divirtieron**
I hope they enjoyed themselves

Temían que **hubiese tenido**/**había tenido** un pinchazo
They were afraid he had had a puncture

c After impersonal constructions unless they express certainty:

No es verdad que **haya habido** una revolución	*It is not true there has been a revolution*
Es importante que le **des** el recado	*It is important you give him the message*
Era improbable que lo **hubiese dicho**	*It was unlikely he said it*
Es una lástima que no **haya visto** la película	*It is a pity he has not seen the film*

but:

Es cierto que les **ha tocado** la lotería	*It is true they have won the lottery*

The impersonal verbs may be followed by an infinitive when used with an object pronoun:

No les importa **saber** de qué color es	*They don't need to know what colour it is*
Le interesa **escuchar** el disco	*She is interested in hearing the record*

16.16 The following cases always have a subjunctive in the dependent clause, regardless of the subject, unless otherwise indicated.

a After doubts, uncertainty and verbs of saying, thinking or remembering used negatively, or in questions when indicating doubt:

Dudo que **sepa** esquiar
I doubt whether he knows how to ski

No dijo que lo **hubiese oído**
He didn't say he had heard it

¿Crees que lo **haya echado** al correo? (doubt)
¿Crees que lo **ha echado** al correo? (neutral question)
Do you think he has posted it?

Statements where the main verb is positive and the verb in the dependent clause is negative are not affected:

Dijo que su padre no le **había escrito**
He said his father had not written to him

similarly clauses dependent on verbs of doubting or denying used negatively:

No negaron que **estaban** enfadados
They did not deny they were annoyed

Tal vez and **quizá** (*perhaps*) may take either the indicative or subjunctive:

Tal vez **sabes** (*or* **sepas**) cómo se llama
Perhaps you know what his name is

b After a negative or indefinite antecedent:

No dijo nada que **fuera** verdad
He didn't say anything that was true

Necesito alguien que **sepa** cocinar
I need someone who can cook
(i.e. anyone will do so long as they can cook)

Busca algo que **quite** esta mancha
He is looking for something (anything) to remove this stain

Los que **quieran** ir al teatro deben presentarse aquí a las ocho
Anyone wanting to go to the theatre must be here at eight

but:

Aquí hay alguien que **sabe** cocinar
Here is someone (definite) who can cook

Tiene algo que **puede** quitar la mancha
He has something (definite) that can remove the stain

Los que **quieren** ir al teatro deben presentarse aquí a las ocho
Those who want to go (i.e. have decided to go) to the theatre must be here at eight

c After certain conjunctions, the commonest of which are listed below:

*para que		*a condición de que	*providing,*
*a fin de que	*in order that,*	con tal que	*on condition that*
de modo que	*so that*	siempre que	
de forma que		a menos que	*unless*
de manera que		a no ser que	
como si	*as if*	*antes (de) que	*before*
cual si		el que	*the fact that*
*sin que	*without*	que	
*en (el) caso que	*in case*	que	*as far as*

(continued over)

*de miedo que	*for fear that*	mientras (que)	*as long as*
no porque	*not because*		

* If the subject of both verbs is the same, these conjunctions may be replaced by the following prepositions + infinitive:

para	sin	de miedo de	antes de
a fin de	en (el) caso de	a condición de	

Iremos al centro para que Vds. **puedan** hacer sus compras
We'll go into the centre so that you can do your shopping

A menos que **haga** buen tiempo, no vale la pena sacar la foto
Unless the weather is fine it is not worth taking the photo

Hágalo antes de que **salgamos**
Do it before we go out

Que yo **sepa**, todavía no ha recibido el paquete
As far as I know, he still has not received the parcel

Ella no compró la camisa de miedo que no le **gustara** a Juan
She didn't buy the shirt for fear that John mightn't like it

but:

Lo trajo **para mostrárselo** a ellos
He brought it to show them

Se fueron **sin decir** nada
They left without saying anything

Normalmente bebe una cerveza **antes de almorzar**
He usually has a beer before having lunch

16.17 Clauses introduced by the following expressions take an indicative when the statement is based on fact or experience and the subjunctive when dealing with future events and hypothetical situations:

a The conjunctions

cuando	*when*	hasta que	*until*
para cuando	*by the time that*	siempre que	*whenever*
después (de) que	*after*	mientras	*while*
en cuanto ⎱		a medida que	*as (time)*
tan pronto como ⎰	*as soon as*	aunque ⎱	
desde que	*since (time)*	ya que ⎰	*although*
cada vez que	*each time that*	a pesar (de) que	*despite*

Cuando **va** a España siempre viaja en avión
When he goes to Spain, he always travels by plane

Mientras **era** estudiante vivía en un apartamento pequeño
While he was a student he lived in a small flat

Aunque **tiene** sus gafas, no puede ver bien
Although he has got his glasses, he cannot see well

but:

Cuando **vayas** a España, no dejes de ir a Granada
When you go to Spain, make sure you go to Granada

Mientras **estés** aquí puedes ayudarme a pintar el cuarto
While you are here you can help me paint the room

Aunque **trabaje** mucho, nunca saca buenas notas
Although he may work hard, he never gets good marks

Note that, if the subject of both verbs is the same, **después (de) que** and **a pesar (de) que** can be replaced by **después de** and **a pesar de** + infinitive:

Nos acostaremos **después de escuchar** las noticias
We will go to bed after listening to the news

A pesar de tener prisa, no tomó un taxi
Despite being in a hurry, he did not take a taxi

b **Por** + adjective/adverb + **que** *however* + adjective/adverb:

Por mucho que se **parezcan**, no son gemelos
However alike they may be, they are not twins

Por lejos que **viva**, siempre llega a tiempo
However far away he may live, he always arrives on time

As this type of construction normally allows for an unlimited degree or quantity of the detail in question, the subjunctive is effectively used in most cases.

c Conjunctions ending in **-quiera** (*-ever*):

comoquiera que	*however, in whatever way*
cualquiera (*plural* cualesquiera) que	*whatever, whichever*
cuando quiera que	*whenever*
dondequiera que	*wherever*
quienquiera (*plural* quienesquiera)	*whoever*

Dondequiera que **va**, la acompaña su perro
Wherever he goes, his dog accompanies him
(It is known exactly where he goes.)

Cuando quiera que **venía**, siempre traía un regalito para la niña
Whenever she came (i.e. every time), she brought a little present for the girl

85

but:

Dondequiera que **vaya**, ...
Wherever he goes (i.e. wherever he may choose to go), ...

Cuando quiera que **vengan**, lo discutiremos
Whenever they come, we will discuss it

16.18 The following type of construction always takes the subjunctive:

sea $\left\{\begin{array}{l}\text{lo que}\\\text{como}\end{array}\right\}$ sea *whatever it may be, be it as it may*

pase lo que pase *come what may*

$\left.\begin{array}{l}\text{diga lo que diga}\\\text{diga lo que quiera}\end{array}\right\}$ *whatever he may say*

beba cuanto beba *however much he may drink*

16.19 Conditions

a Type I

Where the English sentence does not contain a conditional tense (*would, would have*), implying that the condition:

i has been fulfilled, *or*
ii is capable of being fulfilled

here the indicative is used in the **si** clause:

Si no te **gusta** el plato, déjalo
If you don't like the dish, leave it

Si **encuentra** unos tomates baratos, los comprará
If he finds some cheap tomatoes, he will buy them

Si **hacía** sol, ella pasaba todo el día en la playa
If it was sunny, she would spend the whole day on the beach

b Type II

Where the English sentence does contain a conditional tense, implying that the condition is

i hypothetical, *or*
ii incapable of being fulfilled

the **si** clause goes into the subjunctive. A number of variations are possible:

Si $\left\{\begin{array}{l}\textbf{fuera}\\\textbf{fuese}\end{array}\right\}$[1] rico, **compraría**[2] una casa grande

If he were rich, he would buy a large house

[1]Conditional or imperfect subjunctive   [2]Conditional indicative

Si $\left\{\begin{array}{l}\textbf{hubiera sido}\\\textbf{hubiese sido}\end{array}\right\}^1$ rico, $\left\{\begin{array}{l}\textbf{habría comprado}\\\textbf{hubiera comprado}\\\textbf{hubiese comprado}\end{array}\right\}^2$ una casa grande

If he had been rich, he would have bought a large house

[1]Conditional perfect or pluperfect subjunctive

[2]Conditional perfect indicative or subjunctive, or pluperfect subjunctive

Note that when **si** translates *if* or *whether* in reported speech, the indicative is used throughout:

Le preguntaré si **estará** en Roma el martes
I will ask him if he will be in Rome on Tuesday

Le pregunté si $\left\{\begin{array}{l}\textbf{estaría}\\\textbf{había estado}\end{array}\right\}$ en Roma el martes

I asked him if he $\left\{\begin{array}{l}would\ be\\had\ been\end{array}\right\}$ *in Rome on Tuesday*

16.20 Imperative/Command form

a English

Speak, let him/us, etc., *speak* (where this does not request permission).

b Formation

Positive:

tú   the same as 3rd person singular present indicative
vosotros take infinitive, change final **-r** to **-d**
The remainder take the corresponding form of the present subjunctive (16.13a).

habla	come	vive
hable	coma	viva
hablemos	comamos	vivamos
hablad	comed	vivid
hablen	coman	vivan

i   Object pronouns follow the verb and are joined on to it:

Díga**le**   *Tell him*
Cómpra**los**   *Buy them*
Mánda**melo**   *Send it to me*

ii The reflexive form of **nosotros** drops the final **-s** before the pronoun and adds an accent:

Senté**monos**   *Let us sit down*

iii The reflexive form of **vosotros** drops the final **-d** before the pronoun:

Sentaos   *Sit down*

except **irse**:

Idos   *Go away*

-ir verbs require an accent:

Dormíos   *Go to sleep*

Negative:

The present subjunctive is used throughout:

―	―	―
no habl**es**	no com**as**	no viv**as**
no habl**e**	no com**a**	no viv**a**
no habl**emos**	no com**amos**	no viv**amos**
no habl**éis**	no com**áis**	no viv**áis**
no habl**en**	no com**an**	no viv**an**

Object pronouns come before the verb in the normal way:

No **lo** comas   *Don't eat it*
No **los** saquéis   *Don't take them out*

c **Usage**

Basically the same as in English, as in the examples above.
It also appears in certain set expressions:

Oiga *Hey, excuse me*, shouted to a waiter, etc. to attract their attention; or *Hello* said as an introductory remark by a telephone caller.

¿**Diga, dígame?** *Yes, can I help you?* (shop assistant etc., to client); or *Hello* said as an introductory remark by the person answering the phone call.

Tenga *Here you are* (when giving something)

Sírvase *Please* (on generalised written instructions, forms, etc.)

Mande (Mexico) *Sorry/excuse me, I didn't quite catch what you said*

¡**No me digas!** *You don't say!*   ¡**Fíjese/fíjate!** ⎤
¡**Vaya** + noun! *What a (noun)!*   ¡**Figúrese/figúrate!** ⎬*Good heavens!*
                                           ¡**Vaya!** ⎦

d **Note**

i The **él, ella, ellos, ellas** forms are preceded by **que** except in set expressions:

¡**Que** pase!   *Let him come in!*
but:
¡**Viva** el rey!   *Long live the King!*

ii The infinitive is used in generalised commands or instructions:

No **tocar**   *(please) don't touch*
Ver capítulo XX   *see Chapter XX*

iii The infinitive preceded by **a** is sometimes used in conversation as a general exhortation instead of the **nosotros, vosotros** and **Vds.** forms:

Bueno, amigos, ¡a **trabajar!**   *Well, friends, let's get down to work!*
A ver lo que dicen   *Let's see what they say*
¡**A dormir**, chicos!   *Off to sleep, children*

iv The force of the imperative may be softened by using the present indicative:

¿Me **das** diez pesos?   *Could you give me ten pesos?*

Alternative ways of asking someone politely to do something are to preface the request by expressions such as:

¿Me puede/pudiera   ⎫
¿Me hace el favor de   ⎬ + infinitive?
¿Hágame el favor de   ⎭

v The following phrases are also used as commands:

¡Cuidado/ojo!   *Be careful!*   ¡Adelante!   *Come in!*
¡Ánimo!   *Cheer up!*   ¡Fuera!   *Get out!*
¡Silencio!   *Be quiet!*

vi **Vamos a** often translates *let's*:

Vamos a ver (*often just* **a ver**)   *Let's see*
Vamos a comprar un helado   *Let's buy an ice cream*

Vamos on its own or **vámonos** translates *let's go*.

16.21 Continuous tenses (also known as the progressive tenses)

a English

The combination of the verb *to be* with the present participle, e.g.:

I am speaking
I was speaking
I will be speaking, etc.

b Formation

The appropriate tense of **estar** + the present participle, e.g.:

estoy hablando (present)
estaba hablando (imperfect)
estaré hablando (future)

c **Usage**

To emphasise an action that is going on at a precise moment in time, often contrasted with another. To that extent it corresponds with English usage:

¿Qué **estás haciendo**? **Estoy buscando** un número en la guía telefónica.
What are you doing? I am looking up a number in the telephone directory.

Cuando entró **estábamos leyendo** el periódico
When he came in, we were reading the newspaper
(Note that in English there is no difference between the simple and continuous forms of the imperfect.)

d **Note**

i   Even in the above situations this tense tends to be used less than in English.

ii **ir** and **venir** do not have continuous forms:

Va a nevar esta noche
It is going to snow tonight

Ahora **vienen**
They are coming now

iii Unlike English the continuous tenses are not used:

(a) to describe planned future events:

Sale para Nueva York el día veinte
He is leaving for New York on the twentieth

Llegarán a eso de las ocho
They will be arriving at around eight

(b) in letters or on the phone in the following types of expression:

Te **escribimos** para decirte que todavía no hemos recibido tu paquete
We are writing to tell you we still have not received your parcel

Le **devolvemos** el libro que nos prestó
We are returning the book you lent us

Le **habla** Juan Otero
It's Juan Otero speaking

16.22 Infinitive

a This is the form under which verbs are found in dictionaries, etc.: *to speak, to eat*. All Spanish verbs end in **–ar**, **–er**, or **–ir** in the infinitive and are classified accordingly.

For the position of object pronouns with the infinitive see 10.3c.

b Usage

i Directly after certain verbs (list given 19.2):

Desea **pescar** *He wants to fish*
Ella olvidó **fregar** los platos *She forgot to wash up*

ii After a preposition (note that in English the present participle is used, except after *to*):

después de **bajar** del coche *after getting out of the car*
al **cruzar** la calle *on crossing the road*
Trataba de **abrir** la puerta *He was trying to open the door*
una máquina de **escribir** *a typewriter*

iii As a verbal noun (see also 16.24):

Ver es **creer** *Seeing is believing*
Su pasatiempo preferido es *His favourite pastime is playing*
tocar el piano *the piano*
A ella la encanta **hacer** punto *She loves knitting*
el **amanecer** *dawn*
no **fumar** *no smoking*

iv As a translation of the English past participle or passive infinitive in the following types of construction:

Los vi **escribir** *I saw them being written*
Hizo **construir** la casa *He had the house built*
Manda **repartir** el dinero *He is ordering the money to be distributed*

Hemos oído **decir** que es un *We have heard it said he is a very*
abogado muy eficaz *efficient lawyer*
Hace falta **pintar** el comedor *The dining room needs to be painted*
Es de **temer** que . . . *It is to be feared that . . .*

16.23 Perfect infinitive

a English

to have spoken

b Formation

haber + past participle:

haber hablado
haber comido
haber vivido

c **Usage**

As in English, but also where the gerund is used to convey a completed action:

Puede **haber sido** ayer	*It may have been yesterday*
Debe **haber terminado**	*He must have finished*
¿No recuerdas **haber**lo **utilizado?**	*Don't you remember using it?*

16.24 Verbal present participle/gerund

Where the term 'present participle' is used in general terms in this book, it alludes to this verbal form. The adjectival form is explained in 16.25.

a **English**

speaking, e.g.: *he is speaking* or *speaking French is easier than speaking Russian*

b **Formation**

stem + **-ando** (-ar verbs)	hablar	–	hablando
stem + **-iendo** (-er, -ir verbs)	comer	–	comiendo
	vivir	–	viviendo

For the position of the object pronouns used with these forms see 10.3c.

c **Usage**

i   After certain verbs:

(a) **estar** to form the continuous tenses:

Está **subiendo** la escalera
He is going up the stairs

(b) **seguir** and **continuar** when meaning *to continue*:

Sigue **estudiando** la guitarra
He is still studying the guitar

Continuirá **trabajando** en la finca hasta fines de marzo
He will continue to work on the farm until the end of March

Of the two verbs **seguir** is used more frequently.

(c) **ir** meaning *to happen gradually*:

Mientras vayan **subiendo** los precios ...
As/while the prices gradually rise ...

Cuando los chicos fueron **creciendo** ...
When the boys were growing up ...

(d) **llevar**, chiefly in time constructions (18.11):

Llevamos dos meses **viajando** por América Latina
We have been travelling around Latin America for two months

ii When one action is contrasted with another, or complements it, as in the following examples:

Allí están, **mirando** el monumento
There they are, looking at the monument

Regresando de la piscina vimos un incendio
Coming back from the swimming pool we saw a fire

Salió **corriendo**   (see also 18.17)
He ran out

Ella pasó la tarde **charlando** con su amiga
She spent the afternoon chatting to her friend

Nos observaron **recogiendo** la fruta
They watched us picking the fruit

d Note

i When the English present participle really describes a position or completed action, the past participle is used in Spanish (see 16.26):

Están **acostados**
They are lying in bed

ii A present participle used descriptively after a noun in English is normally translated by **que** + the present or imperfect:

La secretaria **que está escribiendo** a máquina en el rincón
The secretary typing in the corner

Tuvimos la habitación **que daba/da** al parque
We had the room overlooking the park

iii The English gerund is frequently translated by an infinitive (see 16.22):

después de **cruzar** la plaza
after crossing the square

Le gusta **pescar**
He likes fishing

or a noun in its own right, when used as such in English:

La pesca es una industria importante
Fishing is an important industry

similarly:

| la equitación | *riding* | las compras | *the shopping* |
| la natación | *swimming* | la calefacción central | *central heating* |

93

iv When the gerund is combined with a possessive or personal pronoun, a clause is usually required in Spanish:

No le gustó **que yo condujera** tan de prisa
He didn't like my driving so fast

¿Le molesta a Vd. **que fume?**
Do you mind him smoking?

El que ella haya muerto no cambiará nada
Her dying will not change anything

16.25 Adjectival present participle

a English

Speaking (as an adjective before a noun – see examples below):

b Formation

stem + **-ante** (**-ar** verbs)	entrar – entrante
stem + **-iente** (**-er**, **-ir** verbs)	correr – corriente
	vivir – viviente
or occasionally + **-ente**:	sorprender – sorprendente

Alternatively, with the exception of the last group, it may be formed by changing the **-do** of the verbal present participle to **-te**.

It agrees like any other adjective (see 7.1–7.3).

c Usage

Limited, except in technical jargon, but always as an adjective:

agua **corriente**	*running water*
la semana **entrante**	*this coming week*
papel **secante**	*blotting paper*
los párrafos **siguientes**	*the following paragraphs*
su cara **sonriente**	*his smiling face*

A dictionary should always be consulted when translating this kind of phrase, as often the Spanish version is totally different:

writing paper	papel de escribir
the dining room	el comedor
a bathing suit	un traje de baño
a tiring day	un día fatigoso

If no adequate adjectival phrase can be found, a clause must be used:

the ripening fruit	la fruta **que está madurando**

16.26 Past participle

a English

spoken

b Formation

stem + **-ado** (**-ar** verbs)   hablado
stem + **-ido** (**-er, -ir** verbs) comido, vivido

In all cases other than (i) below it agrees like any other adjective (7.1–7.3).

c Usage

i In compound tenses (see 16.6, 16.8–16.13) e.g.:

  Ha **encontrado**   *He has found*

ii In the passive:

  La chica fue **educada** en *The girl was educated at a*
  un convento   *convent*

iii It also replaces the English present participle when the relevant action is considered completed:

  Está **sentado**   *He is sitting*
  (i.e. has sat down and has remained sitting)

 as opposed to:

  Está **sentándose**   *He is sitting down*
  (i.e. changing from a standing to a sitting position)

Other common past participles in this category are:

acostado	*lying in bed*	dormido	*sleeping*
apoyado	*leaning*	echado	
arrodillado	*kneeling*	tendido	*lying down*
colgado	*hanging*	tumbado	

iv As an adjective in its own right:

  la torre **construida** en 1810 *the tower built in 1810*
  Fue una clase **aburrida**   *It was a boring lesson*
  Este cuento es **parecido** al *This story is a similar to the*
  otro   *other one*

16.27 Reflexive verbs

a English

I wash myself

b Formation

Reflexive pronoun + verb. Remove **-se** from the infinitive before conjugating:

lavarse   *to wash oneself*

Present tense:

yo me lavo	nosotros nos lavamos
tú te lavas	vosotros os laváis
él, ella, Vd. se lava	ellos, ellas, Vds. se lavan

The only irregularity is the first and second person plural of the positive imperative (16.20b). The position of the reflexive pronoun is explained in 10.3.

c Usage

i True reflexive verbs express an action one does to oneself, whether this is stated in English or not:

Te has cortado	*You have cut yourself*
Ellos se afeitan	*They shave (themselves)*
Ella se despertará	*She will wake up*

They can also be used with parts of the body or clothing (see also 7.9c):

Se ha lavado las manos   *He has washed his hands*

Some verbs exist only in the reflexive, often without any reflexive meaning:

arrepentirse	*repent*	jactarse	*boast*
atreverse	*dare*	quejarse	*complain*
fugarse	*escape*		

ii Reflexive verbs can imply action done to one another:

Se ayudaron	*They helped each other*
Nos aguardaremos	*We will wait for each other*

Sometimes this can be ambiguous:

Se mataron could mean: (a) *They killed themselves*
or: (b) *They killed each other*

This can be clarified or emphasised by adding the following:

oneself, etc.		*each other, etc.*
a* mí mismo	*myself*	(el) uno a(l)* otro
a* ti mismo	*yourself*	(la) una a* la otra
a* sí mismo	$\begin{cases}himself \\ herself \\ yourself \text{ (Vd.)}\end{cases}$	mutuamente recíprocamente
a* nosotros mismos	*ourselves*	
a* vosotros mismos	*yourselves*	
a* sí mismos	$\begin{cases}themselves, \\ yourselves \text{ (Vds.)}\end{cases}$	

    * personal **a** (19.5c), unless a verb takes any other preposition with its object – see examples below:

Se mataron **a sí mismos**	*They killed themselves*
Se mataron **el uno al otro**	*They killed each other*
El niño se acostó **a sí mismo**	*The child put himself to bed*
Se escribirán **mutuamente**	*They will write to each other*
Nos despedimos **el uno del otro**	*We said goodbye to each other*

iii Reflexive verbs may be used to avoid the passive (16.28d):

    Se rompieron dos sillas   *Two chairs were broken*

Certain reflexive verbs have a passive meaning:

llamar	*to call*	but:	llamarse	*to be called*
encontrar $\Big\}$ *to find*			encontrarse $\Big\}$ *to be found,*	
hallar			hallarse	*to be situated*

iv The reflexive pronoun **se** may be used with the third person singular of a non-reflexive verb where the impersonal pronoun *one* or *you* is used in English:

Se puede ir a Africa en barco o en avión	*One can go to Africa by boat or plane*
Se puede aparcar aquí	*You can park here*

But when a reflexive verb is involved **uno** must be used as a subject:

Cuando **uno** se casa joven, . . .	*When one gets married young, . . .*
Si **uno** se despierta temprano, . . .	*If one wakes up early, . . .*

The reflexive pronoun is also used as a deferential form of the first person:

    ¿**Se** puede (pasar)?   *May I come in?*

The reflexive pronoun is sometimes used in impersonal commands:

Véase pág. 73	*See p. 73*
Tradúzcase al francés:	*Translate into French:*

d Note

Many Spanish verbs become reflexive when used without an object. In some cases the reflexive and non-reflexive forms are translated by different verbs in English, for example:

acostar	*to put to bed*	acostarse	*to go to bed*
casar	*to marry (off)*	casarse	*to get married*
detener	*to detain, stop*	detenerse	*to come to a halt, stop*
encender	*to light up*	encenderse	*to catch fire*
enfadar	*to annoy*	enfadarse	*to get annoyed*
levantar	*to raise*	levantarse	*to get up*
sentar	*to seat*	sentarse	*to sit down*
sentir	*to feel (an object)*	sentirse	*to feel (ill, etc.)*
vestir	*to dress (someone)*	vestirse	*to get dressed*

Certain Spanish verbs change their meaning when made reflexive, for example:

beber	*to drink*	beberse	*to drink up*
comer	*to eat*	comerse	*to eat up*
dormir	*to sleep*	dormirse	*to fall asleep*
hacer	*to do, make*	hacerse	*to become**
ir	*to go*	irse	*to go away*
llevar	*to wear, carry*	llevarse	*to take away*
poner	*to put*	ponerse	*to put on, become**
parecer	*to seem*	parecerse	*to resemble*
tratar de	*to try*	tratarse de	*to be a question of*
volver	*to return*	volverse	*to turn, around, become**

* See 18.8.

Others may be used reflexively or non-reflexively without any change of meaning, for example:

bajar(se)	*to get off (vehicles, etc.)*	reír(se)	*to laugh*
parar(se)	*to stop*	sonreír(se)	*to smile*
subir(se)	*to get on (vehicles, etc.)*		

Note the following expressions:

cantar para sí	*to sing to oneself*	leer para sí	*to read to oneself*
hablar para sí	*to talk to oneself*	sonreír para sí	*to smile to oneself*

16.28 The passive

a English

I am spoken to, it is spoken, etc.

b Formation

The appropriate tense of **ser** or **estar** + past participle (which agrees with the subject).

Ser is used for an action in the passive:

La ventana **fue abierta** por María   *The window was opened by María*

Estar is used for the result of an action:

La ventana **estaba abierta** cuando entraste   *The window was open when you came in*

c Usage

i   As in English, but much less frequently in the case of the passive with **ser**:

La chimenea **será limpiada** por la criada	*The chimney will be cleaned by the maid*
El asesino **fue detenido** por la policía	*The murderer was arrested by the police*
Los ejercicios **habían sido corregidos** dos veces	*The exercises had been corrected twice*

ii   *By* is usually translated by **por** as above, but **de** is used after a few verbs:

La reina es amada **de** sus súbditos	*The queen is loved by her subjects*
El general fue seguido **de** otros oficiales	*The general was followed by other officers*
La casa está rodeada **de** árboles	*The house is surrounded by trees*
Siempre ha sido temido **de** sus empleados	*He has always been feared by his employees*

iii   When the passive is used to describe dress, emotions and timing, **ir** is often used as an auxiliary:

Va vestida de luto	*She is dressed in mourning*
Su prima **iba** muy pintada	*His cousin was very made up (literally painted)*
Mi reloj **va** astrasado/adelantado	*My watch is slow/fast*

It is also frequently used with **acompañado** and **incluido:**

Va acompañado de su esposa	*He is accompanied by his wife*
Los impuestos **van incluidos** en el precio	*Taxes are included in the price*

Verse is generally used with **obligado**:

Se vio **obligado** a decírtelo   *He felt obliged to tell you*

d Avoidance of the passive

The passive with **ser** is regarded as a rather clumsy tense in Spanish and is therefore frequently avoided. This may be done in a number of ways:

i If the agent (the originator of the action) is known, the sentence can be changed so that the agent becomes the subject:

El anillo fue encontrado por Conchita
The ring was found by Conchita

changes to:

Conchita encontró el anillo
Conchita found the ring

ii The impersonal *they* can be used:

Fabrican el coche en los Estados Unidos
The car is made in the USA (i.e. *They make the car* . . .)

Le **fusilaron** al prisionero al amanecer
The prisoner was shot at dawn (*They shot* . . .)

The object may be placed in front of the verb to retain the emphasis, but an object pronoun is also needed agreeing with it (10.4e):

El anillo **lo** encontró Conchita
El coche **lo** fabrican en los Estados Unidos
Al prisionero **le** fusilaron el amanecer

iii The reflexive **se** – the verb agrees with what is now the subject:

El museo **se abre** a las tres y media
The museum is opened at half past three (i.e. *The museum opens itself* . . .)

Aquí **se habla** español
Spanish is spoken here (i.e. *speaks itself*)

Se comieron las naranjas
The oranges were eaten (i.e. *ate themselves*)

This form may only be used when referring to things – otherwise an expression like **se mató** could mean *he killed himself* or *he was killed*.

Se may be used with people in the following way:

Se vio a la chica en el mercado
The girl was seen in the market

Se la vio en el mercado
She was seen in the market

To understand the mechanics of this form, the **se** may be thought of as *someone*, i.e. *Someone saw the girl*. The verb, therefore, always goes into the third person singular.

This last form of **se** may be replaced by **uno** or **alguien** (*one/someone*):

> **Alguien** me dijo que lo necesitaba
> *I was told that he needed it (Someone told me . . .)*

iv The passive MUST be avoided in Spanish when using a verb that has an indirect object – the most common examples being verbs of giving, saying, asking, etc.:

> Ramón le dio el cuadro
> *He was given the picture by Ramón (Ramón gave him . . .)*

> Se nos acercaron dos extranjeros
> *We were approached by two foreigners*

> Se le preguntó si tenía algo que declarar
> *She was asked if she had anything to declare*

> Le dijeron que no funcionaba el ascensor
> *He was told that the lift was not working*

v Impersonal constructions in the passive are usually translated in the following ways:

se cree que	*it is believed that*
se dice que	*it is said that*
se sabe que	*it is known that*
se teme que	*it is feared that*
es de creer que	*it is to be believed that*

16.29 Translation of English auxiliaries on their own

a The auxiliaries used to form questions of the following sort are translated by simply ending the Spanish statement with ¿**verdad**? or, more colloquially, ¿**eh**? when expecting a positive or negative reply, and ¿**no**? when expecting a positive reply:

Es cartero ¿**no**?	*He is a postman, isn't he?*
La habitación no da al mar ¿**verdad**?	*The room doesn't look onto the sea, does it?*

similarly:

Hace mucho calor ¿**eh**?	*It's very hot, isn't it?*

b In the first example below the auxiliary is translated by **no**, in the second by **sí**:

Ese reloj está roto; éste **no**	*That watch is broken; this one isn't*
El no rio pero ella **sí**	*He didn't laugh but she did*

c The following type of question is answered by either **sí** or **no** on their own or with a full verb and the appropriate object pronoun. If anything other than a noun object is referred to, **lo** must be used, as in the second and third examples:

¿Leíste la novela? **Sí (la leí).**   *Did you read the novel? Yes, I did.*

¿Cree que los puedan salvar?   *Does he think they can save them?*
No, (no lo cree).   *No, he doesn't.*

¿Eran morenos? **Sí (lo eran).**   *Were they dark haired? Yes, they were.*

d In abbreviated statements after verbs of saying, hoping, fearing, etc., **que sí**, **que no** replace the English auxiliary:

¿Está enferma? Creo **que sí.**   *Is she ill? I think she is.*

¿Vamos a llegar tarde? Espero   *Are we going to arrive late? I hope*
que no.   *we aren't.*

similarly:

¿Es sordo? Claro **que no.**   *Is he deaf? Of course he isn't.*

e In the following cases the Spanish answer simply consists of the subject (unless a full reply is given):

¿Quién va a pagar la cuenta?   *Who is going to pay the bill? He is.*
El (la va a pagar).

In negative answers **no** may be added for contrast:

¿Quién no fue al baile? **Yo**   *Who didn't go to the dance? I didn't.*

but:

Yo **no**, pero ella sí   *I didn't, but she did*

f *So will/do/have/can I etc.* is translated by **yo** etc. **también**:

Tú trabajas como artista. **Ella**   *You work as an artist. So does she.*
también.

Nuestro hijo tiene hambre y **el**   *Our son is hungry and so is theirs*
suyo también

Nor will/do/have/can I etc. is translated by **yo** etc. **tampoco**:

Ellos no compraron nada.   *They didn't buy anything. Nor did I.*
Yo tampoco.

El autobús número 13 no ha   *The no. 13 bus has not passed. Nor*
pasado. **El 6 tampoco.**   *has the 6.*

g When the **gustar** construction (18.7) is being used in (e) and (f) above, the subject pronoun is replaced by **a mí, a ti**, etc.:

¿A quién le encanta la música pop?   *Who likes pop music? I do.*
A mí.

A ella le duelen los pies y **a**   *Her feet are hurting and so are ours*
nosotros también

A is similarly added to any other noun or pronoun in the second statement:

No nos gustó el programa. **A mis**   *We didn't like the programme. Nor*
padres tampoco.   *did my parents.*

17   Irregular Verbs

17.1 Stem change verbs

Verbs in which the last vowel of the stem changes as outlined below.

a Group 1   -AR and -ER verbs

e changes to **ie** ⎫
o changes to **ue** ⎬   when the stress is on the stem
u changes to **ue** ⎭

Parts affected: present indicative and subjunctive, except 1st and 2nd person plural.

pensar	*to think*	encontrar	*to find*	jugar*	*to play*
present	*present*	*present*	*present*	*present*	*present*
indicative	*subjunctive*	*indicative*	*subjunctive*	*indicative*	*subjunctive*
p**ie**nso	p**ie**nse	enc**ue**ntro	enc**ue**ntre	j**ue**go	j**ue**gue
p**ie**nsas	p**ie**nses	enc**ue**ntras	enc**ue**ntres	j**ue**gas	j**ue**gues
p**ie**nsa	p**ie**nse	enc**ue**ntra	enc**ue**ntre	j**ue**ga	j**ue**gue
pensamos	pensemos	encontramos	encontremos	jugamos	juguemos
pensáis	penséis	encontráis	encontréis	jugáis	juguéis
p**ie**nsan	p**ie**nsen	enc**ue**ntran	enc**ue**ntren	j**ue**gan	j**ue**guen

*****Jugar** is the only verb where **u** changes to **ue**. **U** is inserted after the **g** in the present subjunctive to keep the **g** hard before the **e** (1.2a).

b Group 2   -IR verbs

i e changes to **ie** ⎫
    o changes to **ue** ⎬ as in Group 1 above

ii e changes to **i** ⎫
    o changes to **u** ⎬ before **ie**, **ió**, or stressed **a**

Parts affected: present participle; 3rd person singular and plural preterite; 1st and 2nd person plural present subjunctive; imperfect and conditional subjunctive throughout.

preferir	*to prefer*	dormir	*to sleep*
present participle:	pref**i**riendo	*present participle:*	d**u**rmiendo

present indicative	present subjunctive	preterite	present indicative	present subjunctive	preterite
prefiero	prefiera	preferí	duermo	duerma	dormí
prefieres	prefieras	preferiste	duermes	duermas	dormiste
prefiere	prefiera	prefirió	duerme	duerma	durmió
preferimos	prefiramos	preferimos	dormimos	durmamos	dormimos
preferís	prefiráis	preferisteis	dormís	durmáis	dormisteis
prefieren	prefieran	prefirieron	duermen	duerman	durmieron

imperfect subjunctive	conditional subjunctive	imperfect subjunctive	conditional subjunctive
prefiriese, etc.	prefiriera, etc.	durmiese, etc.	durmiera, etc.

c Group 3 –IR verbs

e changes to **i** ⎱ when the stress is on the stem and before **ie**,
o changes to **u*** ⎰ **ió** or stressed **a**

* There are no common verbs in this category.

Parts affected: in all cases where the verbs in Group 2 are affected, namely: present participle; present indicative, except 1st and 2nd person plural; 3rd person singular and plural preterite; present, imperfect and conditional subjunctive throughout.

pedir   *to ask for*

present participle: pidiendo

present indicative	present subjunctive	preterite	imperfect subjunctive	conditional subjunctive
pido	pida	pedí	pidiese, etc.	pidiera, etc.
pides	pidas	pediste		
pide	pida	pidió		
pedimos	pidamos	pedimos		
pedís	pidáis	pedisteis		
piden	pidan	pidieron		

d

Most stem change verbs have to be memorised as such when they are encountered. However, one clue as to whether a verb is in this category is if a stem change has occurred in a noun, etc. related to it which is also stressed on the stem:

almorzar	*to have lunch*	almuerzo	*lunch*
comenzar	*to begin*	comienzo	*beginning*
contar	*to tell a story*	cuento	*short story*
encontrar	*to find*	encuentro	*meeting*
gobernar	*to govern*	gobierno	*government*
helar	*to freeze*	hielo	*ice*

jugar	*to play*	juego	*game*
morir	*to die*	muerte	*death*
nevar	*to snow*	nieve	*snow*
soñar	*to dream*	sueño	*dream, sleep*
volar	*to fly*	vuelo	*flight*

e Other common stem change verbs

Some of these have other irregularities – these are explained in the paragraphs indicated in brackets below. Compound and reflexive forms go like the verbs listed. Some of the more common of these have been included.

Group 1

acordar	*to agree*
acordarse	*to remember*
acostar	*to put to bed*
acostarse	*to go to bed*
almorzar (17.2b)	*to have lunch*
anhelar	*to long for*
apostar	*to bet*
aprobar	*to approve, pass (exam)*
atender	*to attend to*
atravesar	*to cross*
cerrar	*to shut*
colgar (17.2g)	*to hang*
comenzar (17.2b)	*to begin*
contar	*to tell a story*
costar	*to cost*
defender	*to defend*
deshelar	*to thaw*
despertar(se)	*to wake up*
devolver	*to give back*
empezar (17.2b)	*to begin*
encender	*to light up*
entender	*to understand*
envolver	*to wrap up*
gobernar	*to govern*
extender	*to extend*
fregar (17.2g)	*to rub, scrub*
helar	*to freeze*
jugar (17.2g)	*to play*
llover	*to rain*
morder	*to bite*
mostrar	*to show*

106

mover	*to move*
negar (17.2g)	*to deny*
negarse (17.2g)	*to refuse*
nevar	*to snow*
oler (**o** changes to **hue**)	*to smell*
perder	*to lose*
probar	*to try, prove*
recordar	*to remember*
resolver	*to solve*
reventar	*to explode*
regar (17.2g)	*to request*
sentar	*to seat*
sentarse	*to sit down*
soler	*to be accustomed to*
sonar	*to sound, ring (bells)*
soñar	*to dream*
temblar	*to tremble, shake*
tentar	*to attempt*
torcer (17.2d)	*to twist*
tropezar (17.2b)	*to stumble*
verter	*to pour, spill*
volar	*to fly*
volver	*to return*

Group 2

advertir	*to warn*
consentir	*to agree*
divertir	*to amuse*
divertirse	*to enjoy oneself*
herir	*to wound*
hervir	*to boil*
mentir	*to lie*
morir (17.3)	*to die*
preferir	*to prefer*
referir(se)	*to refer*
sentir(se)	*to feel*

Group 3

conseguir	*to obtain*
corregir	*to correct*
despedir	*to dismiss*
despedirse	*to say goodbye*
elegir	*to choose, elect*
freír (17.3)	*to fry*

gemir	*to groan*
impedir	*to prevent*
perseguir (17.2j)	*to pursue, chase*
reír(se) (17.4)	*to laugh*
reñir	*to scold*
repetir	*to repeat*
seguir (17.2j)	*to follow*
sonreír (17.4)	*to smile*
vestir(se)	*to dress*

17.2 Spelling change verbs

These are verbs with spelling changes that follow the rules set out in 1.2a and in some cases also have the odd minor irregularity. The verbs are listed according to their endings.

a –car

c changes to **qu** before **e**

Parts affected: 1st person singular preterite; all of present subjunctive.

buscar   *to look for*

| *preterite:* | bus**qu**é |
| *present subjunctive:* | bus**qu**e, etc. |

b –zar

z changes to **c** before **e**

Parts affected: 1st person singular preterite; all of present subjunctive.

cruzar   *to cross*

| *preterite:* | cru**c**é |
| *present subjunctive:* | cru**c**e, etc. |

c –quir

qu changes to **c** before **a** or **o**

Parts affected: 1st person singular present indicative; all of present subjunctive.

delinquir   *to commit an offence*

| *present indicative:* | delin**c**o |
| *present subjunctive:* | delin**c**a, etc. |

d consonant + **-cer, -cir**

c changes to **z** before **a** or **o**

Parts affected: 1st person singular present indicative; all of present subjunctive.

vencer   *to defeat*

present indicative:	ven**z**o
present subjunctive:	ven**z**a, etc.

e vowel + **-cer, -cir** (for **-ducir**, see (f) below)

add **z** before **-co, -ca**

Parts affected: 1st person singular present indicative; all of present subjunctive.

conocer   *to know*

present indicative:	cono**z**co
present subjunctive:	cono**z**ca, etc.

Some common exceptions:

hacer, decir, satisfacer

f **-ducir**

add **z** before **-co, -ca**

Parts affected: 1st person singular present indicative; all of present subjunctive. They also have an irregular preterite, and consequently imperfect and conditional subjunctive.

traducir   *to translate*

present indicative:	tradu**z**co
present subjunctive:	tradu**z**ca, etc.
preterite:	traduje, traduj**iste**, traduj**o**, traduj**imos**, traduj**isteis**, traduj**eron**
imperfect subjunctive:	traduj**ese**, etc.
conditional subjunctive:	traduj**era**, etc.

g **-gar**

g changes to **gu** before **e**

Parts affected: 1st person singular preterite; all of present subjunctive.

pagar   *to pay*

preterite:	pa**gu**é
present subjunctive:	pa**gu**e, etc.

h -guar

gu changes to **gü** before **e**

Parts affected: 1st person singular preterite; all of present subjunctive.

averiguar   *to find out*
preterite: averi**gü**é
present subjunctive: averi**gü**e, etc.

i -ger, -gir

g changes to **j** before **a** or **o**

Parts affected: 1st person singular present indicative; all of present subjunctive.

proteger   *to protect*
present indicative: prote**j**o
present subjunctive: prote**j**a, etc.

j -guir

gu changes to **g** before **a** or **o**

Parts affected: 1st person singular present indicative; all of present subjunctive.

distinguir   *to distinguish*
present indicative: distin**g**o
present subjunctive: distin**g**a, etc.

k -uir (other than **-guir** and **-quir** above)

i changes to **y** when unaccented and between two or more vowels

construir   *to build*
present participle: constru**y**endo
past participle: construido
present indicative: constru**y**o, contru**y**es, constru**y**e,
                          construimos, construís, constru**y**en
imperfect: construía, etc.
future: construiré, etc.
conditional: construiría, etc.
preterite: construí, construiste, constru**y**ó
                          construimos, construisteis, constru**y**eron
present subjunctive: constru**y**a, etc.
imperfect subjunctive: constru**y**ese, etc.
conditional subjunctive: constru**y**era, etc.
imperative: constru**y**e (tú), construid (vosotros)

110

l -güir

i changes to **y** as above (k)
gü changes to **gu** before **y**

argüir   *to argue*

present participle:	ar**gu**yendo
past participle:	argüido
present indicative:	ar**gu**yo, ar**gu**yes, ar**gu**ye, argüimos, argüís, ar**gu**yen
imperfect:	argüía, etc.
future:	argüiré, etc.
conditional:	argüiría, etc.
preterite:	argüí, argüiste, ar**gu**yó, argüimos, argüisteis, ar**gu**yeron
present subjunctive:	ar**gu**ya, etc.
imperfect subjunctive:	ar**gu**yese, etc.
conditional subjunctive:	ar**gu**yera, etc.
imperative:	ar**gu**ye (tú), argüid (vosotros)

m -eer

i becomes accented whenever stressed
unaccented **i** changes to **y**

Parts affected: participles; imperfect; preterite; imperfect and conditional subjunctive.

creer   *to believe*

present participle:	cre**y**endo
past participle:	creído
imperfect:	creía, etc.
preterite:	creí, creíste, cre**y**ó, creímos, creísteis, cre**y**eron
imperfect subjunctive:	cre**y**ese, etc.
conditional subjunctive:	cre**y**era, etc.

note: both **es** are pronounced separately: cre|er, cre|e, etc.

n -llir, -ñer, -ñir

unstressed **i** is dropped when it follows **ll** or **ñ**

Parts affected: present participle; 3rd person singular and plural preterite; all of imperfect and conditional subjunctive.

	bullir *to boil*	gruñir *to groan*
present participle:	bullendo	gruñendo
preterite:	bulló, bulleron	gruñó, gruñeron
imperfect subjunctive:	bullese, etc.	gruñese, etc.
conditional subjunctive:	bullera, etc.	gruñera, etc.

o **-iar, -uar** (*but not* **-cuar, -guar**)

some of these verbs are stressed on the **i** or **u** when the stress is on the stem

Parts affected: present indicative and subjunctive except 1st and 2nd persons plural.

enviar   *to send*

present indicative:	envío, envías, envía, enviamos, enviáis, envían
present subjunctive:	envíe, envíes, envíe, enviemos, enviéis, envíen

continuar   *to continue*

present indicative:	continúo, continúas, continúa
	continuamos, continuáis, continúan
present subjunctive:	continúe, continúes, continúe,
	continuemos, continuéis, continúen

Other common verbs in this category:

criar	*to bring up, raise*	guiar	*to guide*
enfriar	*to cool down*	liar	*to tie*
espiar	*to spy on*	vaciar	*to empty*
esquiar	*to ski*	variar	*to vary*
fiar	*to trust*	(and compounds)	
actuar	*to act*	situar	*to situate*
efectuar	*to carry out*		

Common verbs NOT in this category:

anunciar	*to announce*	estudiar	*to study*
apreciar	*to appreciate*	financiar	*to finance*
cambiar	*to change*	limpiar	*to clean*
despreciar	*to despise*	negociar	*to negotiate*
divorciar	*to divorce*	odiar	*to hate*
envidiar	*to envy*	pronunciar	*to pronounce*

p The **i** or **u** of the stem of the following verbs is accented as above to separate them from the preceding vowels:

aislar	*to isolate*	reunir	*to reunite*
prohibir	*to prohibit*	rehusar	*to refuse*

present indicative:	aíslo, aíslas, aísla, aislamos, aisláis, aíslan
present subjunctive:	aísle, aísles, aísle, aislemos, aisléis, aíslen
present indicative:	reúno, reúnes, reúne, reunimos, reunís, reúnen
present subjunctive:	reúna, reúnas, reúna, reunamos, reunáis, reúnan

17.3 Common verbs which have irregular past participles but which are otherwise regular:

abrir	to open	abierto
cubrir	to cover	cubierto
describir	to describe	descrito
escribir	to write	escrito
imprimir	to print	impreso
proveer	to provide	provisto
romper	to break	roto

Stem change verbs with irregular past participles:

freír	to fry	frito* (otherwise like **reír**, 17.4)
morir	to die	muerto
resolver	to solve, resolve	resuelto
volver	to return	vuelto

and compounds of both the above groups.

* This form is only used as an adjective:

patatas **fritas**	fried potatoes (chips)

but:

Ha **freído** unas patatas	She has fried some potatoes

17.4 Common irregular verbs

The parts of the verbs given on the following pages are the minimum needed to form all the tenses. For all other parts see Chapter 16.

Verb forms which are irregular are printed in heavy type.

Verbs derived from these irregular verbs behave in the same way, thus, for example, **proponer** (*to propose*) and **suponer** (*to suppose*) go like **poner**. In addition, **satisfacer** (*to satisfy*) goes like **hacer**. Verbs ending in –**dar** and –**ir** do not behave like **dar** and **ir** as they are not true compounds. **Bendecir** (*to bless*) and **maldecir** (*to curse*) have regular past participles, **bendecido** and **maldecido**, but otherwise go like **decir**.

infinitive present participle past participle	present indicative	imperfect	future	conditional
andar *to walk*	regular	regular	regular	regular
caber *to fit* cabiendo cabido	**quepo** cabes cabe cabemos cabéis caben	cabía	**cabré**	**cabría**
caer *to call* **cayendo** caído	**caigo** caes cae caemos caéis caen	caía	caeré	caería
dar *to give* dando dado	**doy** das da damos dais dan	daba	daré	daría
decir *to say* diciendo **dicho**	**digo** dices dice decimos decís dicen	decía	**diré**	**diría**
estar *to be* estando estado	**estoy** **estás** **está** estamos estáis **están**	estaba	estaré	estaría

preterite	present subjunctive	imperfect subjunctive	conditional subjunctive	imperative
anduve	*regular*	**anduviese**	**anduviera**	*regular*
anduviste				
anduvo				
anduvimos				
anduvisteis				
anduvieron				
cupe	**quepa**	**cupiese**	**cupiera**	
cupiste	**quepas**			cabe
cupo	**quepa**			
cupimos	**quepamos**			
cupisteis	**quepáis**			
cupieron	**quepan**			
caí	**caiga**	**cayese**	**cayera**	
caíste	**caigas**			cae
cayó	**caiga**			
caímos	**caigamos**			
caísteis	**caigáis**			caed
cayeron	**caigan**			
di	**dé**	**diese**	**diera**	
diste	**des**			da
dio	**dé**			
dimos	**demos**			
disteis	**deis**			dad
dieron	**den**			
dije	**diga**	**dijese**	**dijera**	
dijiste	**digas**			**di**
dijo	**diga**			
dijimos	**digamos**			
dijisteis	**digáis**			decid
dijeron	**digan**			
estuve	**esté**	**estuviese**	**estuviera**	
estuviste	**estés**			**está**
estuvo	**esté**			
estuvimos	estemos			
estuvisteis	estéis			estad
estuvieron	**estén**			

infinitive present participle past participle	present indicative	imperfect	future	conditional
haber *to have* habiendo habido	**he** **has** **ha** **hemos** habéis **han**	había	**habré**	**habría**
hacer *to do, make* haciendo **hecho**	**hago** haces hace hacemos hacéis hacen	hacía	**haré**	**haría**
ir *to go* **yendo** ido	**voy** **vas** **va** **vamos** **vais** **van**	**iba** **ibas** **iba** **íbamos** **ibais** **iban**	iré	iría
oír *to hear* **oyendo** oído	**oigo** **oyes** **oye** oímos oís **oyen**	oía	oiré	oiría
poder *to be able* **pudiendo** podido	**puedo** **puedes** **puede** podemos podéis **pueden**	podía	**podré**	**podría**
poner *to put* poniendo **puesto**	**pongo** pones pone ponemos ponéis ponen	ponía	**pondré**	**pondría**

preterite	present subjunctive	imperfect subjunctive	conditional subjunctive	imperative
hube	haya	hubiese	hubiera	
hubiste	hayas			he
hubo	haya			
hubimos	hayamos			
hubisteis	hayáis			habed
hubieron	hayan			
hice	haga	hiciese	hiciera	
hiciste	hagas			haz
hizo	haga			
hicimos	hagamos			
hicisteis	hagáis			haced
hicieron	hagan			
fui	vaya	fuese	fuera	
fuiste	vayas			ve
fue	vaya			
fuimos	vayamos			
fuisteis	vayáis			id
fueron	vayan			
oí	oiga	oyese	oyera	
oíste	oigas			oye
oyó	oiga			
oímos	oigamos			
oísteis	oigáis			oíd
oyeron	oigan			
pude	pueda	pudiese	pudiera	
pudiste	puedas			puede
pudo	pueda			
pudimos	podamos			
pudisteis	podáis			poded
pudieron	puedan			
puse	ponga	pusiese	pusiera	
pusiste	pongas			pon
puso	ponga			
pusimos	pongamos			
pusisteis	pongáis			poned
pusieron	pongan			

infinitive present participle past participle	present indicative	imperfect	future	conditional
querer *to want* queriendo querido	**quiero** **quieres** **quiere** queremos queréis **quieren**	quería	**querré**	**querría**
reír *to laugh* **riendo** reído	**río** **ríes** **ríe** reímos reís **ríen**	reía	reiré	reiría
saber *to know* sabiendo sabido	**sé** sabes sabe sabemos sabéis saben	sabía	**sabré**	**sabría**
salir *to go out* saliendo salido	**salgo** sales sale salimos salís salen	salía	**saldré**	**saldría**
ser *to be* siendo sido	**soy** **eres** **es** **somos** **sois** **son**	**era** **eras** **era** **éramos** **erais** **eran**	seré	sería
tener *to have* teniendo tenido	**tengo** **tienes** **tiene** tenemos tenéis **tienen**	tenía	**tendré**	**tendría**

preterite	present subjunctive	imperfect subjunctive	conditional subjunctive	imperative
quise	quiera	quisiese	quisiera	
quisiste	quieras			quiere
quiso	quiera			
quisimos	queramos			
quisisteis	queráis			quered
quisieron	quieran			
reí	ría	riese	riera	
reíste	rías			ríe
rio	ría			
reímos	riamos			
reísteis	riáis			reíd
rieron	rían			
supe	sepa	supiese	supiera	
supiste	sepas			sabe
supo	sepa			
supimos	sepamos			
supisteis	sepáis			sabed
supieron	sepan			
salí	salga	saliese	saliera	
saliste	salgas			sal
salió	salga			
salimos	salgamos			
salisteis	salgáis			salid
salieron	salgan			
fui	sea	fuese	fuera	
fuiste	seas			sé
fue	sea			
fuimos	seamos			
fuisteis	seáis			sed
fueron	sean			
tuve	tenga	tuviese	tuviera	
tuviste	tengas			ten
tuvo	tenga			
tuvimos	tengamos			
tuvisteis	tengáis			tened
tuvieron	tengan			

infinitive present participle past participle	present indicative	imperfect	future	conditional
traer *to bring* **trayendo** traído	**traigo** traes trae traemos traéis traen	traía	traeré	traería
valer *to be worth* valiendo valido	**valgo** vales vale valemos valéis valen	valía	**valdré**	**valdría**
venir *to come* **viniendo** venido	**vengo** **vienes** **viene** venimos venís **vienen**	venía	**vendré**	**vendría**
ver *to see* viendo **visto**	**veo** ves ve vemos veis ven	**veía**	veré	vería

preterite	present subjunctive	imperfect subjunctive	conditional subjunctive	imperative
traje	**traiga**	**trajese**	**trajera**	
trajiste	**traigas**			trae
trajo	**traiga**			
trajimos	**traigamos**			
trajisteis	**traigáis**			traed
trajeron	**traigan**			
valí	**valga**	valiese	valiera	
valiste	**valgas**			vale/**val**
valió	**valga**			
valimos	**valgamos**			
valisteis	**valgáis**			valed
valieron	**valgan**			
vine	**venga**	**viniese**	**viniera**	
viniste	**vengas**			**ven**
vino	**venga**			
vinimos	**vengamos**			
vinisteis	**vengáis**			venid
vinieron	**vengan**			
vi	**vea**	viera	viese	
viste	**veas**			ve
vio	**vea**			
vimos	**veamos**			
visteis	**veáis**			ved
vieron	**vean**			

18 Verbal idioms

18.1 Ser/Estar *to be*

a Use of 'ser'

i Before nouns or pronouns in definitions (i.e. in the question *what, or who, is x?* and the accompanying answer):

¿Quién **es? Es** Nicolás. **Es** él.	*Who is it? It is Nicholas. It is him.*
¿Qué **es** Paco? **Es** un arquitecto estupendo.	*What is Paco? He is a brilliant architect.*
¿Qué **es** esto? No es nada.	*What is it? It's nothing.*

ii Before adjectives or adjectival phrases when describing something permanent or usual (such as nationality, religion, profession, colour, age, materials, ownership, normal character or appearance, etc.) and in questions eliciting such information:

El azúcar **es** dulce	*Sugar is sweet*
El médico **es** francés	*The doctor is French*
El hielo **es** frío	*Ice is cold*
Su barco **es** pequeño	*His boat is small*
La pared **es** roja	*The wall is red*
¿De qué **es** la moneda?	*What is the coin made of?*
Es de plata	*It is made of silver*
¿Cómo **es** la cama?	*How is the bed?*
Es muy cómoda	*It is very comfortable*
Tu abuela **es** vieja	*Your grandmother is old*
Es loca, por eso está en el manicomio	*She's mad, that's why she is in the lunatic asylum*

Note, by comparison with paragraph ii (below) of **estar**, that many adjectives can be used with both verbs depending on the circumstances.

iii Before past participles when describing an action in the passive (16.28):

El palacio **fue** construido en 1597	*The palace was built in 1597*
El colegio **fue** fundado por el Conde de Manzanares	*The college was founded by the Count of Manzanares*

iv With time

Es verano	*It is summertime*
Era de noche	*It was night time*
Son las seis	*It is six o'clock*
Es el 21 de diciembre	*It is 21st December*

v   With numerals:

Dos y tres **son** cinco   *Two and three are five*
La temperatura **es** de 20 grados   *The temperature is 20 degrees*

vi In most impersonal expressions:

es cierto que   *it is certain that*
es que   *the thing is that*
es de creer que   *it is to be believed that*

vii To indicate location – only when *to be* means *to be held* or *take place:*

¿Dónde **es** la fiesta? **Es** en casa   *Where is the party? It's at the*
de los Quiroga.   *Quirogas'.*

b Use of 'estar'

(The numbering of the paragraphs is the same as with **ser**.)

i   Before nouns or pronouns in definitions: NEVER

ii Before adjectives or adjectival phrases describing something unusual, temporary or reversible (for example health, emotions, etc.) and in questions eliciting such information:

¿Cómo **está** la sopa?   *How is the soup?*
Está un poco fría   *It's a bit cold*
Mi café **está** muy dulce   *My coffee is very sweet*
La botella **está** llena   *The bottle is full*
Su marido **estaba** enfermo   *Her husband was ill*
Miguel **está** loco si   *Michael is mad if he wants*
  quiere pagar tanto dinero   *to pay so much money*
Elisa **está** muy vieja hoy   *Elisa is looking very old today*
La criada **estaba** contenta   *The maid was happy*

iii Before past participles describing the result of an action (16.28):

La luz **estaba** apagada   *The light was off*
El bebe **está** dormido ya   *The baby is now asleep*
Los camareros **están** sentados   *The waiters are sitting down*

iv With time – only in the following expression:

¿A cuántos **estamos**?   *What is the date today?*
Estamos a 2 de julio   *It's 2nd July*

v   With numerals – only in the following expression:

¿A cuánto **están** las gambas?   *How much are the prawns?*
Están a 300 pesetas el kilo   *They are 300 pesetas a kilo*

vi Very rarely in impersonal expressions:

Está claro que lo ha olvidado   *It is clear he has forgotten* vii To indicate location (i.e. in the question *where is x?* and the relevant answer):

¿Dónde **está** el cine?	*Where is the cinema?*
Está allí a la derecha	*It is over there on the right*
¿**Está** el obispo?	*Is the bishop in?*

c **Ser** and **estar** may also be used in a number of miscellaneous set expressions:

Ser:

Erase una vez	*once upon a time*
¿Qué **ha sido** de ellos?	*What has become of them?*
¿Cómo **fue** eso?	*How did that happen?*
Sea como **sea**	*Be it as it may* (and similar phrases)
es igual/**es** lo mismo	*It's all the same*
llegar a **ser**	*to turn out, happen, become*

When meaning *to exist*:

Pienso por eso **soy**	*I think therefore I am*
Dios **es**	*God exists*

Before **para** with the idea of purpose:

Las flores **son** para Vd.	*The flowers are for you*
Es para beber ahora	*It is to be drunk now*

Estar:

estar de vacaciones	*to be on holiday*
estar de viaje	*to be travelling*
estar de pie	*to be standing*
estar de rodillas	*to be kneeling*
estar de moda	*to be in fashion*
estar de acuerdo	*to agree*
estar de vuelta	*to be back*
estar de luto	*to be in mourning*
está bien	*it's all right*
¿estamos?	*OK? agreed?*

estar para *to be about to do something; to be in a mood for:*

Está para salir	*He's just about to leave*
No **estamos para** bromas	*We're in no mood for jokes*

estar a punto de *to be just about to do something:*

Están a punto de pagar	*They are just about to pay*

estar por *to have not done something yet; to be in favour of:*

Estoy por terminarlo	*I have not finished it yet*
Estás por vender el coche	*You are in favour of selling the car*

Before the present participle to form the continuous tenses (16.21):

Está cantando	*He is singing*

d A few adjectives have different meanings when used with **ser** and **estar**:

	ser	**estar**
listo	*clever*	*ready*
aburrido	*boring*	*bored*
pesado	*heavy*	*difficult* (person)
malo	*bad*	*ill*
bueno	*good* (by nature)	*well, healthy* (also **bien**)
vivo	*lively, quickwitted*	*alive*
cansado	*tiresome*	*tired*
divertido	*amusing*	*amused*
nuevo	*newly made*	*new, unused*
rico	*rich (wealthy)*	*rich (tasty)*

e A number of common idioms involving the English verb *to be* are translated by other verbs in Spanish. See the following:

hay (18.2, 18.12) **tener** (18.13–18.14)
hacer (18.12) age (14.8)

f **Hallarse** and **encontrarse** may be used instead of **estar** to indicate location:

La plaza de toros **se halla/se encuentra** al final de esta avenida
The bull ring is at the end of this avenue

18.2 Hay *there is, there are* (there is no plural form)

This idiom is a variant of the 3rd person singular present of **haber**. In all other tenses the normal 3rd person singular form of **haber** is used:

Hay un buzón allí	*There is a letter box over there*
Había dos peras sobre la mesa	*There were two pears on the table*
Puede **haber** una pluma en el escritorio	*There may be a pen in the desk*

Hay may never be used before a definite article:

Existe el problema de su pasaporte   *There is the problem of his passport*

Hay is also used in a number of other common expressions:

i   Certain weather idioms (18.12)
ii hay que   *to have to* (18.5)
iii ¿Qué hay?   *How are things? What's up?*
    ¿Qué hay de nuevo?   *What's new?*
iv No hay de qué/No hay por qué   *Not at all, don't mention it*

125

18.3 Poder *to be able*

a English translations of the commoner tenses of **poder**:

present: *is able, can, may*

    Puede hacerlo mañana   *He can/may do it tomorrow*
    Pueden estar enfermos   *They may be ill*

imperfect: *was able, could*

    No lo **podía** alcanzar   *She could not reach it*

future: *will be able*

    ¿**Podrás** estudiar el poema esta   *Will you be able to study the poem this*
    tarde?   *evening?*

conditional: *would be able, could, might*

    Vd. dijo que lo **podría** arreglar   *You said you would be able to fix it*

preterite: *was able, could*

    No **pudimos** avisarle   *We weren't able to let him know*

perfect: *has been able, may/might have*

    Ha podido conseguirlos   *He has been able to get them*
    Podemos haberlo terminado   *We may have finished it*

b The English *can* or *could* is often not translated:

    ¿Me oyes?   *Can you hear me?*

c *May* is often translated by other expressions of possibility

    Es posible que⎫
              ⎬ apruebe el examen   *He may pass the exam*
    Puede que ⎭

    Tal vez ⎧ se levantará⎫
            ⎨   ⎬ temprano   *He may get up early*
            ⎩ se levante ⎭

or by the following requests for permission:

    ¿Me permite?   *May I?*
    ¿Me permite usar el teléfono?   *May I use the phone?*

or more informally:

    ¿Me deja fumar?   *May I smoke?*

and in some cases by the present subjunctive:

    La policía teme que **esté** muerta   *The police fear she may be dead*

126

d Poder means *to be physically able,* **saber** means *to know how to:*

No **puede** jugar al fútbol porque   *He can't play football because he*
se ha roto la pierna   *has broken his leg*
Gloria **sabe** nadar   *Gloria can swim*

18.4 Deber *to have to* (implying moral obligation)

a English translation of the commoner tenses of **deber**:

present: *must, should, ought*

    Debe ayudarle   *He must/should/ought to help him*

imperfect: *had to, was supposed to*

    Debía ayudarle   *He had to help him*

future: *will have to*

    Deberá ayudarle   *He will have to help him*

conditional: *should, ought* (stronger than present)

    Debería ayudarle   *He really should help him*

preterite: *had to, was obliged to*

    Debió ayudarle   *He had to help him*

perfect: *has had to, must have*

    Ha debido ayudarle   *He has had to help him*
    Debe haberle ayudado   *He must have helped him*

b Deber also means *to owe:*

    Me **debes** cien pesos   *You owe me 100 pesos*

c Deber de is used to translate *must,* etc. in the case of assumptions:

    Salieron de Santiago a las once,   *They left Santiago at eleven, so*
    así que **deben de** haber llegado   *they must have arrived*

In practice **deber** on its own is often used with this meaning.

18.5 Tener que + infinitive *to have to* (neutral necessity)

In impersonal constructions **hay que** is used instead. Often this hides a personal usage, like the English *one:*

    Tuvimos que abrir la ventana   *We had to open the window*
    porque hacía tanto calor   *because it was so hot*

Creo que **tuvieron que enviar** un telegrama	*I think they had to send a telegram*
No sabían cuánto **había que pagar**	*They did not know how much to pay*
¿**Hay que entregar** el pasaporte?	*Does one have to surrender one's passport? (Do I/we . . .)*

18.6 Haber de *to be to, it is arranged that*

| **Habéis de ir** a buscarles a mediodía | *You are to go and fetch them at midday* |
| ¿Qué **he de hacer**? | *What am I to do?* |

It can also mean the same as **deber de** or **tener que**, but this usage tends to be rather literary:

| **Han de ser** les tres | *It must be three o'clock* |

18.7 Gustar *to like*

a In the case of **gustar** and verbs like it the English subject becomes an indirect object and the English object becomes the subject, the verb agreeing with it. The word order is normally still basically the same as in English:

| **Me** gusta la motocicleta | *I like the motorbike (i.e.: The motorbike is pleasing to me)* |
| ¿**Te gustan** las manzanas? | *Do you like the apples?* |

b **Gustar más** may be used instead of **preferir** *(to prefer):*

| ¿Cuál **te gusta más**, el vino blanco o el vino tinto? | *Which do you prefer, white wine or red?* |
| **Me gusta más** la cerveza | *I prefer beer* |

c There are other common Spanish verbs which use this construction:

i encantar *to like very much, love, be delighted with*

| **Les encanta** dibujar | *They love drawing* |
| A ella **le encantan** esas faldas | *She loves those skirts* |

ii faltar – when meaning *to be lacking, be short of, need*

| ¿Cuánto dinero **os falta**? | *How much money are you short of?* |
| **Me faltan** tres botones | *I need three more buttons* |

128

iii hacer falta   *to need* (for a purpose)

Nos hace falta asegurar el
equipaje

We need to insure the luggage

Te hacen falta unas zanahorias
para el guisado

You need some carrots for the stew

iv quedar   *to be left*

Nos quedan cuatro días aquí

We have got four more days here

Le quedan mil dólares

He has got a thousand dollars left

v doler   *to hurt, ache*

Me duele el brazo izquierdo

My left arm aches

Le duelen los dientes

His teeth ache

vi interesar   *to be interested in*

No **nos interesan** las noticias

We are not interested in the news

vii importar   *to mind*

No **les importa** la demora

They do not mind the delay

18.8 *To become* + adjective or noun;
to get/go/grow/turn + adjective

There is no single translation for the verb *to become*, etc., but the following is a
guide to the most frequent ways of expressing this in Spanish:

a + noun:

through one's effort: **hacerse**

Se hará dentista

He will become a dentist

Se han hecho amigos

They have become friends

as a matter of course: **llegar a ser**

Llegó a ser general a los 50 años

He became a general at 50

indicating a change of nature: **convertirse en, transformarse en**

Torremolinos **se ha convertido
en** un centro turístico muy
importante

*Torremolinos has become a very
important tourist resort*

Este castillo **se ha transformado
en** un hotel de alta categoría

This castle has become a first class hotel

expressions of time: **hacerse**

Se está haciendo tarde

It is getting late

expressions of age: **llegar a tener, tener, cumplir**

Cuando $\begin{cases} \textbf{llegue a tener } 50 \text{ años} \dots \\ \textbf{tenga } 50 \text{ años} \dots \\ \textbf{cumpla } \text{los } 50 \text{ años} \end{cases}$ *When he turns 50 . . .*

b + adjective:

deliberately: **hacerse**

> **Se hizo** rica *She became rich*

emotionally or physically – a quick, temporary change: **ponerse**

> **Se ponen** nerviosos *They become nervous*
> **Te has puesto** rojo *You have gone red*
> **Nos pusimos** enfermos *We got ill*

as before, but more slowly or with lasting effect: **quedarse**

> **Se han vuelto** locos *They have gone mad*
> **Se quedará** ciego *He will go blind*
> **Te estás quedando** sordo *You are going deaf*

but in many cases such expressions can be translated by a verb formed from the adjective. Sometimes these are formed by adding a suffix like **-ecerse** or **-ar** (**se**) to the stem of the adjective, in many other cases the prefix **en-, em-,** or **a-** is also required, for example:

mejorarse	*to get better*	enfadarse	*to get annoyed*
mojarse	*to get wet*	enloquecerse	*to go mad*
calentarse	*to get warm*	alargarse	*to get longer*
enriquecerse	*to get rich*	empeorar	*to get worse*

There are also other verbs that have this meaning when made reflexive, such as:

confundirse	*to get confused*	casarse	*to get married*
cansarse	*to get tired*	perderse	*to get lost*
aburrirse	*to get bored*	vestirse	*to get dressed*

18.9 *To make someone/something* + noun or adjective

There are numerous ways of translating this into Spanish. Many involve the non-reflexive forms of the verbs used in the previous section:

> Ese negocio no te **hará** rico *That business will not make you rich*
> El plato les **ha puesto** enfermo *The dish has made them ill*
> Vamos a **convertir** esta calle **en** *We are going to make this street a*
>   una zona peatonal   *pedestrian precinct*
> La multa le **enfadó** mucho *The fine made him very angry*

| El policía **te puso** muy nervioso, ¿no? | The policeman made you very nervous, didn't he? |
| Todo este trabajo me **cansaría** pronto | All this work would soon make me tired |

18.10 Hacer + infinitive *to have/get something done; to make someone do something*

Hacemos arreglar el coche	We are having the car repaired
Harán instalar una piscina	They will have a swimming pool installed
Eso le **hizo reír** a carcajadas	That made him laugh his head off
Les **hicimos callar** a los niños	We got the children to keep quiet

When someone else is being made to do something, **hacer** can be followed by **que** + subjunctive:

| **Haré que** me **contesten** pronto | I will get them to reply quickly |

If the action is being done to or for oneself a reflexive verb can often be used:

| El **se cortará** el pelo | He will get his hair cut |
| Ella **se ha hecho** un vestido | She has had a dress made for her |

Note also the following expressions:

hacer entrar	to show (someone) in
hacer subir	to show (someone) up
hacer esperar	to keep (someone) waiting

18.11 Translations of *for* and *since* in time constructions

a	desde	since (preposition)
	desde que	since (conjunction)
	desde cuando	since when, how long (past)
	desde hace	
	hace (*time*) que	for (time leading up to a particular moment, either now or in the past)
	llevar (*time*) + present participle	

With all these constructions, when an action begun in the past continues into the present, the present is used in Spanish:

El ascensor funciona **desde** ayer
The lift has been working since yesterday

Desde que está en Inglaterra, ha aprendido mucho inglés
Since he has been in England, he has learnt a lot of English

Están esperando la llamada **desde hace** una hora
They have been waiting for the phone call for an hour

The last type of expression may also be rendered in the following ways:

Hace una hora **que** esperan la llamada
Llevan una hora esper**ando** la llamada

and the question eliciting this answer may be put in one of three ways:

¿**Desde cuándo** están esperando la llamada?
¿**Cuánto tiempo hace que** están esperando la llamada?
¿**Cuánto tiempo llevan** esper**ando** la llamada?
How long have they been waiting for the phone call?

The *constructions involving* **desde hace/desde cuando** and **hace que** are the ones most commonly used.

b When the pluperfect (*had been*) is used in the English sentence, the imperfect is used in the main clause in Spanish, providing the action was incomplete at the time the second action took place. **Hace** changes to **hacía**:

Hacía dos horas **que** trabajaba cuando entré

or:

Trabajaba **desde hacía** dos horas cuando entré
He had been working for two hours when I went in

c When the first action is completed before or when the second action takes place, the same tenses are used as in English:

Habían estado en Alemania **desde hacía** cinco años cuando estalló la guerra

or:

Hacía cinco años **que** habían estado en Alemania cuando estalló la guerra
They had been in Germany for five years when war broke out
(implying that they then left)

This often applies to sentences with a negative meaning:

Hace dos meses **que** no hemos ido al teatro
We have not been to the theatre for two months

Dijo que **hacía** tres días **que** no había podido dormir bien
He said he had not been able to sleep well for three days

d Hace also translates *ago* and precedes the unit of time:

Ocurrió **hace unas semanas**	*It happened a few weeks ago*
El bebe nació **hace seis meses**	*The baby was born six months ago*

e **Durante** translates *for* (duration of an action or state), alternatively the preposition can be omitted:

La charla duró más de una hora	*The talk went on for more than an hour*
Ha tenido fiebre (**durante**) tres días	*He has had a temperature for three days*
Estarán una semana en Asunción	*They will be in Asunción for a week*

Durante can also mean *during*:

durante la Semana Santa	*during Holy Week*

f **En** translates *for*, as above (e), but where an action has not taken place or is not expected to:

No les visitó nadie **en** cinco días	*Nobody visited them for five days*
No saldrá del hospital **en** una semana	*He won't be leaving hospital for a week*

g **Para** translates *by*, *for* a specific point in time (see also 19.13):

La cita era **para** las diez	*The appointment was for ten o'clock*
Esta composición es **para** el lunes que viene	*This essay is for next Monday*
Ha vuelto **para** el cumpleaños de su hija	*He has come back for his daughter's birthday*

Para can also mean *for* after actions carried out for the purpose of spending time somewhere or using something for a period of time:

Se lo prestaré **para** una semana	*I will lend it to him for a week*
Lo necesitarías **para** quince días	*You would need it for a fortnight*
Han venido aquí **para** un mes	*They have come here for a month*

18.12 Weather

a Some verbs exist in their own right:

* helar	*to freeze*	lloviznar	*to drizzle*
* deshelar	*to thaw*	* tronar	*to thunder*
* llover	*to rain*	relampaguear	*to lighten*
* nevar	*to snow*	granizar	*to hail*

* These verbs belong to the stem change group (17.1).

No llueve ahora	*It is not raining now*
Nevaba ayer	*It was snowing yesterday*

b Many expressions are made up of **hacer** or **hay** with a noun. **Hacer** is normally used when there is no visible object:

¿Qué tiempo hace?	*What is the weather like?*
Hace buen tiempo	*It is fine*
Hace mal tiempo	*The weather is bad*
Hace buen día	*It is a fine day*
Hace mal día	*It is a foul day*
Hace calor	*It is hot*
Hace frío	*It is cold*
Hace fresco	*It is chilly*
Hace viento	*It is windy*
Hace 20 grados	*It is 20°*
Hace 5 grados bajo cero	*It is −5°*

but also: Hace sol `It is sunny*

Hay is normally used with a clearly visible object:

Hay luna	*The moon is shining*
Hay neblina	*It is misty*
Hay niebla	*It is foggy*
Hay polvo	*It is dusty*
Hay lodo	*It is muddy*
Hay tempestad	*It is stormy*
Hay nubes	*It is cloudy*

c In all the above expressions **mucho** translates *very* and **tanto** translates *so* or *as*. Both words agree with the noun as usual:

Hace **mucho** calor	*It is very hot*
Habia **mucha** niebla anoche	*It was very foggy last night*
No hace **tanto** frío ahora	*It is not cold now*
No hay **tantas** nubes como antes	*It is not as cloudy as before*

d **Estar** is used in isolated idioms:

Está nublado	*It is cloudy*
Está oscuro	*It is dark*

18.13 Other expressions involving heat and cold

a With people and animals: **tener calor/frío**

Tengo calor	*I am hot*
El perro tiene frío	*The dog is cold*

Mucho and **tanto** are used as in 18.12c;

Tenía mucho frío	*He was very cold*
El gato tendrá tanto calor	*The cat will be so hot*

b With objects (always or usually hot/cold): **ser caliente/frío**
(of variable temperature): **estar caliente/frío**

El sol **es** caliente	*The sun is hot*
El hielo **es** frío	*Ice is cold*
El café **está** muy caliente	*The coffee is very hot*
La cerveza **está** fría	*The beer is cold*

18.14 Further idioms with 'tener'

Tener is used before a number of other nouns where the English phrase is made up of *to be* + adjective, etc.:

tener cuidado	*to be careful*
tener la culpa	*to be guilty*
tener éxito	*to be successful*
tener gracia	*to be funny*
tener hambre (*fem.*)	*to be hungry*
tener sed (*fem.*)	*to be thirsty*
tener miedo	*to be afraid*
tener prisa	*to be in a hurry*
tener razón (*fem.*)	*to be right*
tener sueño	*to be sleepy*
tener buena suerte	*to be lucky*
tener mala suerte	*to be unlucky*

18.15 Some idiomatic uses of 'dar' (*to give*)

dar a	*to look onto*
dar con	*to bump into*
dar de comer	*to feed*
No me da la gana	*I don't feel like it*
dar un grito dar voces	*to shout, scream*
Me da igual Lo mismo me da	*It's all the same to me*
dar la hora	*to strike the hour*
Dan las seis	*It is striking six*
dar un paseo dar una vuelta } *en el coche* '*car outing*'.	*to go for a stroll*
¡qué más da!	*too bad, never mind*
darse cuenta de	*to realise*
darse prisa	*to hurry up*

135

18.16 Some other common verbs that present translating problems

a *appear*

to come into view: **aparecer**

Apareció a la ventana	*He appeared at the window*

to seem: **parecer**

Pareces algo preocupado	*You appear a little worried*

b *ask*

to ask questions: **preguntar**

Le preguntó qué tenía en su maleta	*He asked him what he had in his suitcase*

The full expression for *to ask a question* is **hacer una pregunta**.

to ask for/after someone: **preguntar por**

Están preguntando por el gerente	*They are asking for the manager*

to ask for something (order): **pedir**

Pedí un bocadillo de jamón	*I asked for a ham sandwich*

to ask someone to do something: **pedir**

Le pidieron que se lo mostrara	*They asked him to show it to them*

to ask more formally (to request): **rogar**

Se ruega a los señores pasajeros no fumar	*Passengers are kindly asked not to smoke*

c *change*

to change money, exchange: **cambiar**

¿Se pueden cambiar dólares aquí?	*Can one change dollars here?*

to alter: **cambiar**

¿Puede Vd. cambiar la hora de la cita?	*Can you change the time of the appointment?*

to change trains, clothes, mind, etc.: **cambiar de**

Tienes que cambiar de tren en Irún	*You must change trains in Irún*
Se va a cambiar de camisa	*He is going to change his shirt*

d *give*

to give (generally): **dar**

Les dimos las llaves   *We gave them the keys*

to give as a present: **regalar**

La regalará un collar para su   *He will give her a necklace for*
cumpleaños   *her birthday*

to give in (i.e. *hand in*): **entregar**

Hay que entregar el trabajo hoy   *The work must be given in today*

e *have*

before a past participle in compound tenses: **haber**

Ha comido   *He has eaten*

possession, etc.: **tener**

Su hermana tiene una bicicleta   *His sister has a bicycle*

when meaning to eat or drink: **tomar**

Vamos a tomar una copa de vino   *We are going to have a glass of wine*

f *know*

to know people, animals, places, familiar objects: **conocer**

¿Conoces Buenos Aires?   *Do you know Buenos Aires?*
Ella conoce a tu madre   *She knows your mother*

to know facts/how to do something: **saber**

Sé cuánto cuesta   *I know how much it costs*
La chica sabe cocinar   *The girl knows how to cook*

g *leave*

to go out of: **salir** (**de** + noun)

Salen de la oficina   *They leave the office*

to go away (people): **irse, marcharse**

Se fue sin decir nada   *He left without saying anything*

to go away (trains, etc.): **salir**

El autobús sale de allí   *The bus leaves from over there*

to leave somebody/something somewhere: **dejar**

Lo dejaré en la mesa   *I will leave it on the table*

to leave unchanged, etc.: **dejar**

Lo dejamos así   *We'll leave it like that*

Déjale en paz   *Leave him in peace*

h *love*

to love people: **querer** (**amar** is rarely used nowadays)

La quiere a Elena   *He loves Elena*

to love objects/doing something: **encantar, gustar mucho** or **muchísimo**
(18.7)

Le encanta la muñeca   *She loves the doll*

Les encanta esquiar   *They love skiing*

Nos gustaría mucho ir al baile   *We would love to go to the dance*

i *play*

to play games: **jugar** (**a** + definite article)

Juegan al baloncesto   *They play basketball*

to play music: **tocar**

Toca el violín   *He plays the violin*

j *put*

to place (generally): **poner**

Póngalo aquí   *Put it here*

to put with care/precision: **colocar**

Coloqué el vaso al lado del otro   *I put the glass next to the other one*

to put inside: **meter**

Lo había metido en un cajón   *He had put it in a drawer*

k *return*

to go back: **volver, regresar**

Han vuelto de Cozumel   *They have returned from Cozumel*

Regresaremos pronto   *We will return soon*

to give back: **devolver**

Devolvieron el paraguas hace
poco   *They returned the umbrella a
short while ago*

l *spend*

to spend money: **gastar**

Hemos gastado mil pesos   *We have spent a thousand pesos*

to spend time: **pasar**

Van a pasar quince días en Grecia   *They are going to spend a fortnight in Greece*

m *take*

to take (most senses): **tomar**

Tome dos píldoras por día   *Take two pills a day*
Tome la primera bocacalle a la   *Take the first turning on the right*
derecha

to take people/things somewhere: **llevar**

Te llevará a la estación   *He will take you to the station*

to take away: **llevarse**

Se ha llevado dos botellas   *He has taken away two bottles*

to take photographs: **sacar** (also **hacer**)

Sacaré una foto del puerto   *I will take a photo of the harbour*

to take out: **sacar**

Saca su pañuelo del bolsillo   *He takes his handkerchief out of his pocket*

n *think*

to believe: **creer**

Creen que se han perdido   *They think they have got lost*

to think (generally): **pensar**

Piensa mucho pero dice poco   *He thinks a lot but says little*

to think of (intend): **pensar**

Pensamos comprar otro coche   *We are thinking of buying another car*

to think of (have an opinion): **pensar de**

¿Qué piensas de la actriz?   *What do you think of the actress?*

to think of (have in one's thoughts): **pensar en**

Está pensando en su novia   *He is thinking of his girlfriend*

18.17 Translation of English verbs needing a preposition or adverb to complete their meaning

a The prepositions or adverbs used fall into three categories:

i Those which completely change the original meaning of the verb:

  *put **up with*** (tolerate)   *run **out of*** (have no more)

ii Those which are used idiomatically but which do not alter the basic meaning of the verb:

  *open **up** = open*   *cover **over** = cover*

iii Those which add to the original meaning of the verb in a consistent way:

  *go **back**, fly **back**, run **back***

Note that some idioms can fall into more than one category, thus *run out of* used figuratively belongs to group i, but used literally (*to leave fast*) belongs to group iii.

For the first group a dictionary is usually the only guide, unless one knows the translation for a synonym consisting of an unqualified verb, i.e. **aguantar** = *to put up with* and *to tolerate*.

In the case of the second, the translation of the idiom and the unqualified verb is usually the same, thus **abrir** = *to open* and *to open up*, and **cubrir** = *to cover* and *to cover over*.

The most usual Spanish way of dealing with the last group is to find a verb that conveys the force of the English preposition or adverb and then qualify it with a present participle, adverb or adverbial phrase.

It should be noted that the examples given below are a guide to the ways of translating these phrases rather than general rules.

b **Translation of the commonest idioms in category iii**

English prep. or adverb	Usage	Spanish key element	Examples
away	motion	alejarse, salir	*to swim away:* alejarse nadando *to hurry away:* salir de prisa
	continuity	seguir, continuar	*to burn away:* seguir quemando *to drink away:* continuar bebiendo
	removal	quitar	*to blow away:* quitar soplando
across	motion	cruzar	*to jump across:* cruzar de un salto *to fly across:* cruzar volando (*birds*), cruzar en avión (*plane*)

140

English prep. or adverb	Usage	Spanish key element	Examples
back	motion (no object)	volver, regresar	*to limp back:* volver cojeando
			to sail back: regresar en barco
	(+ object)	devolver	*to give (take/put/bring/hand) back*
down	motion	bajar	*to rush down:* bajar apresuradamente
			to look down: bajar la vista
in/into	motion	entrar	*to ride in:* entrar cabalgando
	insertion	meter	*to put in:* meter empujando
off	motion	alejarse	*to walk off:* alejarse andando
	removal	quitar	*to rub off:* quitar frotando
on	continuity	seguir, continuar	*to sing on:* seguir cantando
			to read on: continuar leyendo
out	motion (no object)	salir	*to drive out:* salir en coche
	removal	sacar	*to take/bring out*
over	motion	cruzar	*to crawl over:* cruzar arrastrándose
through	motion	atravesar	*to cycle through:* atravesar en bicicleta
up	motion	subir	*to run up:* subir corriendo
			to dash up: subir de prisa
	completion	... (lo) todo	*to eat up:* comer (lo) todo
			to sell up: vender (lo) todo
		... completamente	*to fill up:* llenar completamente
		... por completo	*to finish up:* terminar por completo
	emphasis	various	*to dress up:* vestir(se) elegantemente
			to cut up: cortar en pedazos

note:

When the verbs *to go* and often *to bring, take, step, come* and *walk* are used in this way, all that is required in Spanish is one verb. For example:

bajar = *to go (come/walk/step/take/bring) down*

Hacer and **dejar** can be combined with many verbs of motion with the following effect: **hacer** *to cause something or somebody to move in a given direction*; **dejar** *to let something or somebody move in a given direction.* Thus:

hacer subir   *to force up*   dejar entrar   *to let/allow in*

19 Prepositions

As in English prepositions are often required as link words after verbs, adjectives and nouns. In many cases these are the same in both languages, for instance:

quejarse de	*to complain of*	rico en	*rich in*
empezar por	*to begin by*	el miedo de	*the fear of*

19.1 A guide to prepositions used after verbs

a Prepositions required before a dependent verb

a + infinitive

Verbs of beginning and certain related verbs:

comenzar a		aprender a	*to learn to*
empezar a	*to begin to*	disponerse a	*to get ready to*
ponerse a		ayudar a	*to help to*
echarse a		forzar a	*to force to*
apresurarse a	*to hurry to*		

Ella ayudó a su abuelo **a** incorporarse en la cama
She helped her grandfather sit up in bed

Verbs of motion when expressing purpose:

Salen **a** comer
They are going out to eat

Vino **a** felicitarte
He came to congratulate you

Certain verbs of repetition:

volver a   *to do something again*

de + infinitive

Verbs of finishing:

terminar de	
cesar de	*to finish*
dejar de	
acabar de	*to have just (done something)*

Terminan **de** trabajar a las seis
They stop working at six

por + infinitive

Verbs of beginning/finishing by:

empezar, etc. por *to begin by*   terminar, etc. por *to finish by*

La orquesta empezó el concierto **por** tocar un vals
The orchestra began the concert by playing a waltz

The following types require no preposition before a dependent infinitive:

Verbs of influence, such as those of advising, making, ordering, wanting, preventing, permitting, needing:

aconsejar	*to advise*	preferir	*to prefer*
hacer	*to make*	impedir	*to prevent*
mandar	*to order*	permitir	*to allow*
querer	*to want*	necesitar	*to need*

Quiero comprar unas postales
I want to buy some postcards

Verbs of the senses:

ver *to see*   oír *to hear*   sentir *to feel*

Vimos nadar a Juan
We saw John swim

Verbs in the **gustar** group (18.7) and other impersonal verbs:

No le gusta ir de compras con su hermana
He doesn't like going shopping with his sister

Basta decir que estaba de muy mal humor
Let's just say he was in a very bad mood

b Prepositions required before either another verb or an object

de

Verbs indicating emotional reactions:

alegrarse de	*to be glad about*
avergonzarse de	*to be ashamed of*
gozar de	*to enjoy*
enamorarse de	*to fall in love with*
hartarse de	*to be/get fed up with*
preocuparse de	*to worry about*

Su hija se ha enamorado **de** un joven policía
His daughter has fallen in love with a young policeman

Verbs of disassociation:

abstenerse de	*to abstain/refrain from*
prescindir de	*to do without*
olvidarse de	*to forget* (but no preposition after **olvidar**)
carecer de	*to lack*

El sereno se ha olvidado **de** traer las llaves
The nightwatchman has forgotten to bring the keys

c Prepositions required before an object

a
Verbs of approaching:

acercarse a ⎱	
aproximarse a ⎰	*to approach*
sentarse a	*to sit down at*
arrimarse a	*to lean against*

¿Todavía no se han sentado **a** la mesa?
Haven't they sat down at the table yet?

Verbs of resemblance or comparison:

parecerse a	*to resemble*
comparar a	*to compare with*
saber a	*to taste of*
oler a	*to smell of*

La sopa huele **a** ajo
The soup smells of garlic

de
Verbs of separation:

alejarse de ⎱	
apartarse de ⎰	*to move away from*
despedirse de	*to say goodbye to*
mudarse de	*to move (houses), change*

Los niños se despidieron **de** sus amigos desde el balcón
The boys said goodbye to their friends from the balcony

Verbs of filling, covering, etc. with:

cargar de	*to load with*
llenar de	*to fill with*
cubrir de	*to cover with*

El camión estaba cargado **de** heno
The lorry was laden with hay

d **Common verbs that require a preposition in English but that take a direct object in Spanish**

aguardar ⎫ esperar ⎭	to wait for
escuchar	to listen to
pedir	to ask for
aprovechar	to profit from, take advantage of
buscar	to look for
tirar	to throw away

Las campesinas están esperando el autobús
The peasant women are waiting for the bus

19.2 A list of common verbs showing what preposition, if any, they take before another verb or noun:

abstenerse de *to abstain, to refrain from*
aburrirse de *to get bored with*
acabar con *to put an end to*
acabar de *to have just*
acabar por *to finish by*
acercarse a *to approach*
acertar a *to manage to*
aconsejar *to advise*
acordarse de *to remember, to agree to*
acordarse con *to agree with*
acostumbrarse a *to get accustomed to*
acusar de *to accuse of*
advertir de *to notify, warn*
aficionarse a *to grow fond of*
aguardar a *to wait until*
alegrarse de *to be glad*
alejarse de *to move away from*
amenazar con *to threaten with*
anhelar *to long to*
animar a *to encourage*
apartarse de *to move away from*
apelar a *to resort to*
apresurarse a *to hurry to*
aprobar *to approve of*
aprender a *to learn to*
aprovecharse *to take advantage of*
aproximarse a *to approach*
arrimarse a *to lean against*

asemejarse a *to resemble*
asistir a *to be present at*
asomarse a *to appear at*
asomarse por *to lean out of*
asombrarse de *to be surprised at*
asustarse de *to be frightened at*
atreverse a *to dare to*
avergonzarse de *to be ashamed of*
ayudar a *to help to*
bajar de *to get off/out of vehicles*
burlarse de *to make fun of*
cansarse de *to tire of*
carecer de *to lack*
cargar de *to load with*
casar a *to marry off*
casarse con *to get married to*
cesar de *to stop (doing)*
chocar con *to crash into*
comentar *to comment on, discuss*
comenzar a *to begin to*
comparar a *to compare to*
comparar con *to compare with*
conducir a *to lead to*
conseguir *to succeed in*
consentir en *to agree to*
consistir en *to consist of*
constar de *to consist of*
consultar con *to consult*

145

contar con *to rely, count on*
contestar a *to reply to*
convenir a *to suit (people)*
convenir en *to agree to*
convenir con *to agree with*
convidar a *to invite to*
creer *to believe*
dar a *to look onto*
dar con *to run across*
darse cuenta de *to realise*
deber de *to have to* (18.4)
decidir *to decide*
dejar *to allow, let*
dejar de *to stop (doing)*
depender de *to depend on*
desear *to desire to*
despedirse de *to say goodbye to*
detenerse a *to stop to*
detestar *to hate*
dirigirse a *to head for*
disponerse a *to get ready to*
echar(se) a *to begin to*
elegir *to elect, choose to*
empezar a *to begin to*
empezar por *to begin by*
enamorarse de *to fall in love with*
encontrarse con *to meet*
enfadarse de *to get annoyed with*
  (things)
enfadarse con *to get annoyed with*
  (people)
enojarse de *to be angry with (things)*
enojarse con *to be angry with (people)*
enseñar a *to teach how to*
enterarse de *to find out about*
entrar en *to enter*
equivocarse de *to be wrong about*
escuchar *to listen to*
esperar a *to wait until*
estar a punto de *to be on the point of*
estar de acuerdo con *to agree with*
evitar *to avoid*
examinarse en *to take an exam in*
fiarse de *to trust*
fijarse en *to notice*
fingir *to pretend to*

forzar a *to force to*
gozar de *to enjoy*
haber de *to be to* (18.6)
hablar con *to talk to*
hacer caso a *to pay attention to*
hacer daño a *to harm*
hartarse de *to be/get fed up with*
impedir *to prevent*
inquietarse de *to worry about*
intentar *to try to*
interesarse en *to be interested in*
invitar a *to invite to*
jugar a *to play* (18.16i)
lograr *to succeed in, manage to*
luchar por *to struggle to, strive for/to*
llegar a *to reach*
llenar de *to fill with*
mandar *to order to*
merecer *to deserve*
mirar *to look directly at*
mirar a *to look towards*
mudarse de *to change, move (house)*
necesitar *to need*
negar *to deny*
negarse a *to refuse to*
obligar a *to oblige to*
ocuparse de *to take care of, attend to*
ofrecer *to offer to*
oler a *to smell of*
olvidar *to forget*
olvidarse de *to forget*
oponerse a *to be opposed to*
ordenar *to order to*
parar de *to stop (doing)*
parecer *to seem*
parecerse a *to resemble*
pedir *to ask for (things)* (18.16b)
pensar en/de *to think of* (18.16n)
permitir *to allow to*
persuadir a *to persuade to*
poder *to be able* (18.3)
ponerse a *to start to*
preferir *to prefer*
preguntar por *to ask for (people)*
  (18.16b)
preocuparse de *to worry about*

probar a *to try to*
prohibir *to prohibit*
prometer *to promise*
prepararse a *to prepare to*
proponer *to propose*
quedar en *to agree to*
quedar por *to remain to be* (done)
quedarse a *to remain/stay to*
quejarse de *to complain of*
recordar *to remember*
referirse a *to refer to*
reírse de *to laugh at*
reparar en *to notice*
resistir a *to resist*
resultar *to turn out, result*
retirarse a *to retire to*
rodear de *to surround with*
rogar *to request*
romper a *to suddenly start to*
saber *to know how to* (18.3d)
saber a *to taste of*
salir de *to leave*
sentarse a *to sit down to/at*
subir(se) a *to get on/into vehicles*
sentir *to feel, sense, regret*
servir de *to serve as*
servir para *to be good for*

servirse de *to use*
soler *to be used to*
sonreírse de *to smile at*
soñar con *to dream of*
sorprenderse de *to be surprised at*
tardar en *to take time (doing)*
temer *to fear*
tener ganas de *to want to*
tener miedo de *to be afraid of*
  (things)
tener miedo a *to be afraid of (people)*
tener que *to have to* (18.5)
tentar a *to try to*
terminar por *to end by*
tirar de *to pull*
trabajar de *to work as*
trabajar en *to work at*
trabajar por/para *to work to/for*
traducir a *to translate into*
tratar de *to try to*
tratarse de *to be a question of*
trepar a *to climb into*
trepar por *to climb along*
tropezar con *to run across*
vacilar en *to hesitate in*
vestirse de *to be dressed as*
volver a *to return to; do again*

In some cases an alternative preposition is allowed after these verbs without any change in meaning or function, for example:

alegrarse con, de *or* por   *to be glad about*
preocuparse de *or* por   *to worry about*

19.3 Verbs taking two objects

In the case of many verbs taking two objects (or an object and a clause) the person becomes the indirect object. This is nearly always true anyway of verbs of communicating (telling, advising, asking, etc.) or giving:

Va a decir la verdad **al juez**
He will tell the judge the truth

Le aconsejamos **a tu primo** que saliese temprano
We advised your cousin to leave early

Ha mostrado su pasaporte **al policía**
He has shown the policeman his passport

Ella le pidió **a su amiga** que le ayudara
She asked her friend to help her

19.4 Prepositions after adjectives and nouns

a Where an infinitive is considered the subject of a verb, no preposition is used before it:

Es fácil hacerlo	*It is easy to do it*
Es imposible leer con este ruido	*It is impossible to read with this noise*
Resultó difícil terminarlos a tiempo	*It proved difficult to finish them on time*
Es una lástima tener que regresar a la oficina	*It is a pity to have to return to the office*

b Otherwise a preposition is always used. The commonest is **de**:

Esta novela es difícil **de** leer	*This novel is difficult to read*
Gonzalo es capaz **de** ser muy eficaz	*Gonzalo is capable of being very efficient*
¿Me hace el favor **de** firmar aquí?	*Could you please sign here?*
Los ganadores estaban locos **de** alegría	*The winners were mad with joy*

c The preposition used is often the same as that following a related verb, for example:

parecido a	*similar to*	(parecerse a)
dispuesto a	*ready to*	(disponerse a)
rodeado de	*surrounded by*	(rodear de)
obligado a	*obliged to*	(obligar a)
la lucha por	*the struggle to*	(luchar por)

note also:

de

after superlatives:

Es la mejor habitación **del** hotel	*It is the best room in the hotel*

con

attitude towards:

Está furioso **con** ellos	*He is furious with them*
Estaba severo **con** sus estudiantes	*He was severe with his students*

para con is sometimes used, especially after **bueno** and **malo**:

El patron fue muy bueno **para**   *The boss was very good towards*
con sus empleados   *his employees*

en

ability at something:

Eres bueno/fuerte **en** matemáticas   *You are good at maths*
Es malo **en** biología   *He is bad at biology*

between **primero**, **último** and **único** and infinitive:

Fue el primero/último/único **en**   *He was the first/last/only one*
llegar   *to arrive*

19.5 A

a General uses

to, onto

a ti	*to you*
a Madrid	*to Madrid*
a la izquierda	*to/on the left*
Cayó **al** suelo	*It fell onto the floor*
Pegó el sello **al** sobre	*He stuck the stamp onto the envelope*
Ella añadirá leche **al** café	*She will add milk to the coffee*

at (time)

a la una	*at one*
a los trece años	*at the age of thirteen*
a veces	*at times*
a fines del año	*at the end of the year*

similarly:

a tiempo	*on time*
al día siguiente	*the next day*

at/by (next to/distance but not *in*)

a la puerta	*at the door*
a orillas del mar	*by the seaside*
a 10 km de aquí	*10 km from here*

at (rate)

a 50 k.p.h.	*at 50 k.p.h.*
tres veces **al** mes	*three times a month*

at (price)

a 200 ptas. el kilo	*at 200 ptas. a kilo*

in (weather, etc.)

al sol	*in the sun*
al viento	*in the wind*
a la sombra	*in the shade*

but:

bajo la lluvia	*in the rain*

from people (after verbs of removal, purchase, hiding, etc.)

Le robaron £500 **al sastre**	*They stole £500 from the tailor*
¿**A quién** compraste la bicicleta?	*From whom did you buy the bicycle?*
El chico escondió el juguete **a su hermano**	*The boy hid the toy from his brother*

before objects of verbs of the senses used in conjunction with another verb:

Vemos **al** pájaro volar en el cielo	*We can see the bird flying in the sky*
Oíste decir **al** mecánico que estaba roto	*You heard the mechanic say it was broken*

in certain adverbial expressions, such as:

a mi ver	*in my opinion*	a caballo	*on horseback*
al teléfono	*on the telephone*	a lo lejos	*in the distance*
a ciegas	*blindly*	al contrario	*on the contrary*
a pie	*on foot*	poco a poco	*little by little*

b Al + infinitive

on/while (doing something), etc.

Chocó con el camión **al cruzar** la avenida	*He crashed into the lorry as he was crossing the avenue*
Al llegar al aeropuerto, alquilamos un coche	*On arriving at the airport we hired a car*

c Personal 'a'

A is placed before specific people or domestic animals when they are the direct object of a verb:

La bala hirió **al** soldado	*The bullet wounded the soldier*
La chica echa de menos **a** su caballo	*The girl misses her horse*

but:

Buscamos una cocinera	*We are looking for a cook* (any cook)
Detesta los abogados	*He hates lawyers* (lawyers in general)

150

It is not used after **tener** in its usual meaning of *to have, possess*:

Tiene cuatro hijos   *He has got four children*

It is optional

i   before words beginning with **a**:

No conoces **(a) Arturo**   *You do not know Arthur*

ii   in sentences where there is also an indirect object:

Llevará **(a) su madre** al médico   *He will take his mother to the doctor*

iii before personified abstract nouns (it is generally only inserted in literary Spanish):

Ama **(a) la paz**   *He loves peace*

iv before expressions of quantity or collective nouns:

Invitaremos **(a) veinte personas**   *We will invite twenty people*
El alcalde alabó **(a) la policía**   *The mayor praised the police*

19.6 Antes de, delante de, ante

a Antes de

before (time)

antes de la una   *before one o'clock*
antes de viernes   *before Friday*

b Delante de

before (in front of)

Estaban de pie **delante de** la   *They were standing before the*
puerta   *door*

c Ante

before (in the presence of, faced with)

El prisionero comparecerá **ante**   *The prisoner will appear before*
el juez   *the judge*
No se puede hacer nada **ante** esa   *One cannot do anything when faced*
situación   *with that situation*

19.7 De

of

los guantes **de** la vieja	*the old woman's gloves*
(The *'s* construction does not exist in Spanish.)	
una botella **de** coñac	*a bottle of brandy*
tres **de** los gatos	*three of the cats*

in numerous other such adjectival phrases:

un collar **de** perlas	*a pearl necklace*
el avión **de** Quito	*the Quito plane*
el hijo **de** ocho años	*the eight year old son*
un edificio **de** diez pisos	*a ten storey building*

miscellaneous expressions:

de acuerdo	*O.K.*	de veras	*really*
de prisa	*in a hurry*	de pie	*standing*
de moda	*in fashion*	ir de compras	*to go shopping*
de repente	*suddenly*	pintar de blanco	*to paint white*

from (see also: **a** (19.5), **desde** (19.9))

el turista **de** Italia	*the tourist from Italy*
Llegaron **de** la ciudad	*They arrived from the town*
de vez en cuando	*from time to time*
Data **del** siglo XVI	*It dates from the 16th century*

of, about

Hablan **de** religión	*They are talking about religion*

19.8 Debajo de, bajo

under, below

debajo de is used more frequently in the physical sense:

La cesta está $\left\{\begin{array}{l}\textbf{debajo de}\\\textbf{bajo}\end{array}\right\}$ la mesa   *The basket is under the table*

bajo is always used in the figurative sense or with temperatures:

bajo el gobierno democrático	*under the democratic government*
dos grados **bajo** cero	*two degrees below zero/minus two*

19.9 Desde

from a point (with verbs of seeing, calling, throwing, etc.)

Le llamaron **desde** el comedor
They called him from the dining room

Podemos ver la catedral **desde** el primer piso
We can see the cathedral from the first floor

Los chicos estaban tirando piedras **desde** el puente
The boys were throwing stones from the bridge

desde tu punto de vista
from your point of view

from (onwards)

Desde Granada el paisaje era más interesante
From Granada onwards the countryside was more interesting

from . . . to (usually to emphasise distance or time)

desde las tres hasta las cinco
from three to five

Durmió en el tren **desde** Toledo hasta Cuenca
He slept in the train all the way from Toledo to Cuenca

since (see also 18.11)

desde ayer
since yesterday

19.10 En

in (or *at* = *in*)

en el camión	*in the lorry*
en el hospital	*at/in the hospital*
en vano	*in vain*
en paz	*at/in peace*
en 1900	*in 1900*
en 15 minutos	*in 15 minutes*
en voz baja	*in a low voice*

(*but*: llegar **a** *to arrive in*;   salir **a** *to go out into*)

For expressions of weather – see 19.5a.

into

Entra **en** el vestíbulo	*He goes into the hall*
Metí la mano **en** el bolsillo	*I put my hand in(to) my pocket*

by (transport)

en avión	*by plane*
en autobús	*by bus*

(see also: **por** 19.14)

at (time – occasionally)

en este momento	*at this moment*
en aquella época	*at that time*

on (place)

en el baúl	*on the trunk*
en el suelo	*on the ground*
en el tercer piso	*on the third floor*

To avoid any confusion in the use of **en** (*on* or *in*), one can use **encima de** (*on top of, above*):

Los platos están **encima del** horno	*The plates are on top of the stove*

or **sobre** (*on, above*):

La ropa está **sobre** la cama	*The clothes are on the bed*

Miscellaneous expressions such as:

en cuanto	*as soon as*
en seguida	*immediately*
en cambio	*on the other hand*
lavar en seco	*to dry clean*

19.11 Hacia

towards

El sereno se dirige **hacia** la puerta	*The night watchman is heading for the door*

Hacia may be combined with the following to convey motion in a particular direction: **arriba** (*above*), **abajo** (*below*), **adelante** (*in front*), **atrás** (*behind*), **adentro** (*inside*), **afuera** (*outside*), for example:

hacia arriba	*upwards*	hacia afuera	*outwards*
hacia atrás	*backwards*	hacia adentro	*inwards*

around (time)

hacia las once	*at around eleven*

(*alternatively:* **a eso de** ..., **sobre** ...)

19.12 Hasta

until, up to (time)

hasta julio	*until July*
hasta ahora	*up to now*

as far as

Siga **hasta** el semáforo	*Go straight on as far as the traffic lights*

up to (numerically)

Asistieron **hasta** sesenta personas	*Up to sixty people attended*

even, including

Hasta ellos se asombraron	*Even they were surprised*

19.13 Para

for (purpose, destination, use, suitability)

la llave **para** el coche	*the key for the car*
un regalo **para** su novia	*a present for his girl friend*
Sale **para** Venezuela	*He is leaving for Venezuela*
¿**Para** qué necesitas tanto dinero?	*What do you need so much money for?*
apto **para** el empleo	*suitable for the job*
útil **para** el jardín	*useful for the garden*

by, for a future moment (see also 18.11g)

Se fijó la reunión **para** el día diez	*The party was arranged for the tenth*
Para cuando regreses ya estará listo	*By the time you return it will be ready*

for (bearing in mind, etc.)

Hace mucho frío **para** mayo	*It is very cold for May*
Es muy grande **para** sus años	*He is very tall for his age*
Es muy malo **para** la salud	*It is very bad for one's health*

Miscellaneous expressions:

para siempre	*for ever*
para empezar	*to start with*
leer para sí	*to read to oneself* (16.27d)

155

19.14 Por

along, through, around, about (motion)

Anduvimos **por** el sendero	*We walked along the path*
Pase **por** aquí	*Come along here/Step this way*
El tren pasa **por** el túnel	*The train goes through the tunnel*
Lanzó un ladrillo **por** la ventana	*He threw a brick through the window*
Viajarán **por** Francia	*They will travel through France*
Vaga **por** la ciudad	*He is wandering around the town*

Por is also combined with the following to convey motion:

encima de	*on top of, above*	**por** encima de	*over*
debajo de	*under*	**por** debajo de	*under*
delante de	*in front of*	**por** delante de	*past*
detrás de	*behind*	**por** detrás de	*behind*
entre	*between, among*	**por** entre	*through, between*
donde	*where*	**por** donde	*the way that, along which, by way of which*
¿dónde?	*where?*	¿**por** dónde	*which way?*

El buzón está delante de la farmacia	*The letter box is in front of the chemist's*
El joven corrió **por delante de la** puerta de la panadería	*The lad ran past the bakery door*
Los libros están debajo del escritorio	*The books are under the desk*
El coche va a pasar **por debajo del** puente	*The car is going to go under the bridge*
Tu abrigo está entre el de él y el mío	*Your coat is between his and mine*
El sol brillaba **por entre** las hojas	*The sun was shining through the leaves*
¿Dónde está el postre?	*Where is the dessert?*
¿**Por dónde** vinieron Vds.?	*Which way did you come?*
La carretera **por donde** vinieron es muy mala	*The road along which they came is very bad*

in, around, etc. (vague location)

La carta debe estar **por** allí	*The letter must be over there somewhere*
Había polvo **por** todas partes	*There was dust everywhere*
¿Hay un hotel **por** aquí?	*Is there a hotel near here?*

in, around, etc. (time – usually vague)

por la mañana	*in the morning*
por aquel entonces	*at around that time*

por Navidad   *at Christmas time*
(It is not used with time of the clock – see **hacia** 19.11.)

by, per, etc. (rate)

100 km **por** hora	*100 km per hour*
un veinte **por** ciento	*twenty per cent*
cinco veces **por** hora	*five times an hour*
Perdieron **por** dos a uno	*They lost by two to one*

by (passive – 16.28)

El tabaco fue descubierto **por**   *The tobacco was discovered by*
    el aduanero   *the customs officer*

by (by means of)

por correo aéreo	*by airmail*
llamar **por** teléfono	*to telephone*
por barco	*by boat*

(In Spain **por** is normally used for freight, **en** for passengers)

Lo obtuvo **por** un amigo   *He got it through a friend*

for, because etc. (cause, reason)

por eso	*for that reason*
¿**por** qué?	*why, for what reason?*
Han ido **por** leche	*They have gone to get some milk*
No viene **por** estar enferma	*She is not coming because she is ill*
por lo que dicen	*judging by what they say*

for (exchange)

Mi hermano me dio 200 pts. **por**   *My brother gave me 200 pts. for*
    el disco   *the record*
Lo puede cambiar **por** otro   *You can change it for another one*
Los vecinos pagan cincuenta mil   *The neighbours are paying £50,000*
    libras **por** la casa   *for the house*

but **por** is omitted if no price is mentioned:

Pagaba la comida   *He was paying for the meal*

for (considered equivalence)

por ejemplo	*for example*
Les dejaron **por** muertos	*They left them for dead*
Le tienen **por** listo	*He is thought to be clever*

for (feelings)

No siente nada **por** ellos   *He feels nothing for them*

however + adjective or adverb

por muchos que haya   *however many there may be*
     (see 16.17b)

to, to be + infinitive (action to be completed)

cuentas **por** pagar   *bills to be paid*
postales **por** escribir   *postcards to be written*
(see also 18.1c)

for (for the sake of, in favour of, for the benefit of, on behalf of, instead of)

por amor de Dios   *for the love of God*
Lo haremos **por** ti   *We will do it for you*
Vota **por** el partido   *He votes for the party*
hablar **por** hablar   *to talk for the sake of talking*
Contestaré **por** ella   *I will reply on her behalf*

Numerous miscellaneous expressions:

por fin	*finally, at last*	por una parte	*on the one hand*
por lo menos	*at least*	por desgracia	*unfortunately*
por casualidad	*by chance*	por supuesto	*of course*
por completo	*completely*	por lo visto	*apparently*
por escrito	*in writing*	por mí	*as far as I'm concerned*

19.15 Según

according to

Según el pastor va a llover mañana
According to the shepherd it will rain tomorrow

as (progression)

Según avanzábamos nos sentíamos cada vez más cansados
As we walked on we felt more and more tired

as, just as

El cuarto está **según** lo dejó
The room is just as he left it

19.16 Sobre

on (place – see also **en** 19.10)

Las cucharas están **sobre** el mantel
The spoons are on the tablecloth

El mural **sobre** esa pared es de Diego Rivera
The mural on that wall is by Diego Rivera

on, about (concerning)

Hay una conferencia **sobre** Fidel Castro a las dos
There is a lecture on Fidel Castro at two

above, over

El cuadro está **sobre** el aparador
The picture is above the sideboard

El avión voló **sobre** el mar
The plane flew over the sea

quince grados **sobre** cero
five degrees above zero

about (approximately)

Santiago tiene **sobre** cuatro millones de habitantes
Santiago has about four million inhabitants

El curso termina **sobre** el 18 de diciembre
The course finishes about 18 December

La película empieza **sobre** las siete y media
The film starts at about half past seven

19.17 General Observations

a Spanish prepositions must always come before the word they qualify:

la señora **con** quien habla	*the lady he is talking with*
¿**De** qué se trata?	*What is it about?*

b Any prepositions required after verbs and nouns, etc., are usually retained when followed by a dependent clause:

Aguarda **a** que venga	*Wait until he comes*
Nos alegramos **de** que se haya casado	*We are glad he has got married*
Tiene miedo **de** que suceda otra vez	*He is afraid of it happening again*

20 Conjunctions not covered elsewhere

20.1 And

addition:

y

Pedro **y** María   *Peter and Mary*

e before words beginning with **i** or **hi** and no vowel following

padre **e** hijo   *father and son*
alemanes **e** ingleses   *Germans and English*

but:

acero **y** hierro   *steel and iron*

combination:

con
    pan **con** mantequilla   *bread and butter*
    whisky **con** soda   *whisky and soda*

purpose (see 19.1a):

    Se sentó **a** leer el periódico   *He sat down and read the paper*
    Ven **a** verme esta tarde   *Come and see me this afternoon*
    Trate **de** conducir con más   *Try and drive more carefully*
    cuidado

both ... and   **tanto ... como**

    Tanto los peruanos **como** los   *Both Peruvians and Bolivians*
    bolivianos hablan español   *speak Spanish*

20.2 Or

o

    jueves **o** viernes   *Thursday or Friday*

An accent is needed between numerals: 2 **ó** 3   *2 or 3.*

u before words beginning with **o** or **ho**

siete **u** ocho	*seven or eight*
mujeres **u** hombres	*women or men*

either . . . or   **o** . . . **o**

O está estudiando en la biblioteca	*Either he is studying in the library*
o ha salido a comer	*or he has gone out to eat*

20.3 Que

Que translates *that* before both phrases and clauses introduced by verbs of saying, etc., and cannot be omitted as it can in English:

Dijo **que** tenías razón	*He said (that) you were right*
¿Cuándo abren otra vez? Me imagino **que** a las tres.	*When do they open again? At three, I imagine.*

Similarly it may not be omitted when introducing a relative clause (see also 10.7):

Las peras **que** compraron son deliciosas	*The pears (which) they bought are delicious*

20.4 Porque

Porque (*because*) should not be confused with **por qué** (*why*).

Como (*as*) should be used instead of **porque** at the beginning of a sentence:

Tomás está en casa **porque** tiene fiebre	*Thomas is at home because he has a temperature*
Como hacía frío me puse un suéter	*Because/As it was cold, I put a sweater on*

A causa de translates *because of:*

La fábrica está cerrada **a causa de** la huelga	*The factory is closed because of the strike*

21 Inversion

a Spanish word order is much more flexible than English. It is not uncommon to find the subject placed after the verb or the object placed before the verb for emphasis or other stylistic reasons, for example:

No lo quiere **nadie**	*Nobody wants it*
El plato lo rompió **Miguel**	*Michael broke the plate*

b The subject always follows the verb after direct speech:

– ¿Dónde te duele? – **preguntó el médico.**	*'Where does it hurt?' the doctor asked.*

c One should avoid ending a subordinate clause with a verb if at all possible:

No saben **a qué hora llegará el tren**	*They don't know at what time the train will arrive*
¿Has olvidado **dónde está el mercado?**	*Have you forgotten where the market is?*

d Note the usefulness of the personal **a** construction (19.5c) in distinguishing between a subject and an object in these situations:

Mientras esperaba su madre ...	*While his mother was waiting ...*
Mientras esperaba **a** su madre ...	*While he was waiting for his mother ...*

Index

References are to paragraph numbers, or chapters where no sub-section is given. Where a number of references are made, the main ones appear in heavy type.